INFIDELITY

Exploding the Myths

This edition first published 2013

Bay Road Media,
16 Kenyon Ave, Mt Eden, Auckland 1024, New Zealand.
www.bayroadmedia.com

Copyright© Julia Hartley Moore 2013
Julia Hartley Moore asserts the moral right to be identified as the author of this work.

All rights reserved. Except for short extracts for the purpose of review, no part of this book may be reproduced, stored in a retrieval system or transmitted in any form or by any means. This includes electronic, mechanical, photocopying, recording or otherwise, without prior written permission from the publisher.

ISBN 978-0-473-26823-7

Text design and production by ebooklaunch.com
Cover design by ebooklaunch.com
Cover photograph by Nicki Maud Photography

INFIDELITY

Exploding the Myths

JULIA HARTLEY MOORE

CONTENTS

Acknowledgements 9
Introduction 11
Chapter 1: Dispelling the myths of infidelity 21
Chapter 2: Julia's story: Part 1 53
Chapter 3: Signs of betrayal 65
    Intuition 67
    The signs 67
    Denials and excuses 84
    Stupid excuses 89
Chapter 4: Women are their own worst enemies 93
    Virtue—a blessing or a curse? 108
    Guilt trip 110
    Leave it to the professionals 112
    Intimidation tactics 113
    Covering his tracks by taking advantage
of female sensibilities 116
Chapter 5: Human nature is a curious thing 119
    One minute he's there and then he's gone 124
    Men who leave with somewhere
and someone to go to 125
    Girl power 129
    The revenge affair 130
    Friends and allies 136
    Who's the boss? Wives who blame the other woman and

confront her Boundaries 137
    Boundaries 139
    Male boundaries 145
Chapter 6: Julia's story: Part 2 149
Chapter 7: A word to the guys 161
    For all those philanderers out there 164
    Let's talk about control 167
    The link between porn and infidelity 169
    What it is that women want? 171
Chapter 8: Men are their own worst enemies 173
    Facing the truth 175
    When men are betrayed 181
Chapter 9: When you live with a liar 185
    Danger! Danger! 190
Chapter 10: Julia's story: Part 3 193
Chapter 11: How to spot a cheat at 1000 paces 205
    Actions speak the truth, not words 207
    When someone shows you
who they are, believe them 208
    There is no smoke without fire 210
    Wandering eyes 210
    Beware of the wolf in sheep's clothing 211
    Financial betrayal 223
    Internet infidelity 236
    Financial love cheats on the net 242
    Predators on the net 244
Chapter 12: How to have an affair 255
    The rules 258
    Mistresses beware 268
Chapter 13: Women who leave 271
    Suzy's story 273
Chapter 14: Most frequently asked questions 293

Chapter 15: Turn the wounds into wisdom 303
    Prevention is better than cure 305
    Respect, trust, love and commitment 314
Chapter 16: Julia's story: Epilogue 319

ACKNOWLEDGEMENTS

Thanks to the fabulous Alison Brook of Bay Road Media for believing in this book and its message. Thanks to Brent and also Gillian – you know who you are and you know how valuable your contributions have been! A special thank-you must go to my thousands of clients over the years; it's been a privilege working for you, and without your stories this book could never have been written.

I especially want to thank my family and friends for putting up with me while I was working on this book, but you should be used to it by now – you are all saints! And lastly, a very special thank-you to my husband Steve, for being a wonderful sounding board and source of support and for bringing true happiness to my life.

Please note that the language in this book is often gender-specific to men, but applies to all, regardless of gender, race and sexual orientation. Men are highlighted as a gender not because all men betray or all betrayers are men; it's because they tend to be caught more than women do – and most of my clients are women. It should also be noted that I have not used actual names or exact circumstances in the stories featured in this book, in order to protect the privacy of individuals involved.

Julia Hartley Moore

INTRODUCTION

How can the person you trust the most in the world betray you? How can the one you love above all others break your heart? How can someone you care about more than anything not care about you?

These are questions that millions of people around the world have had to ask themselves. Even people as famous as Sandra Bullock, Elin Nordegren and Robert Pattinson.

The sad reality is that with every relationship and every marriage comes the possibility of infidelity. It doesn't matter how rich, beautiful, powerful, successful or intelligent you are – infidelity doesn't care. Infidelity doesn't discriminate; infidelity couldn't care less where you live, what you drive, what career path you've chosen, what religion you practice, what your ethnic background is. No matter what gender you are, whether you are straight, gay or bi, or what political affiliations you have, infidelity can find you.

I'm not a psychologist, I'm not a professor; I don't deal in theories. I'm a private investigator, and I deal in cold hard facts – what I know about infidelity I've learned at the coal face of betrayal; I see the shattered lives, the broken families, the grief that infidelity leaves in its wake.

Infidelity can strike at any time with a force so powerful that it leaves you incapable of functioning. It contaminates your waking thoughts and makes sleep impossible. In fact, experts tell us that to live with such stress levels for a prolonged period can reduce our life expectancy by 10 to 14 years. As far as I'm concerned, that on its own is reason enough to write this book.

So what is infidelity? Well, most of us think of it as someone having a physical relationship with a person other than their partner, but it's actually a lot more complicated than that. There are two kinds of infidelity – physical and emotional – but what they have in common is that infidelity by its nature always involves deception. And that's why infidelity really, really hurts.

Physical infidelity usually means having covert sexual relations with somebody who is not your partner. But to some people it isn't as straightforward as that – as former US president Bill Clinton famously tried to argue when he told the world, "I did not have sexual relations with that woman!" Monica Lewinsky may have performed oral sex on Bill, but in his book a blowjob is not sex, so he wasn't cheating on his wife Hillary at all. How would that sit with you?

Emotional infidelity can cause just as much hurt, pain and suffering as physical infidelity, if not more. Emotional infidelity is usually thought of as getting too emotionally close to someone who isn't your partner. It could be an extended flirtation with someone you don't want your partner to know about, which might involve long lunches, constant text messaging or intimate exchanges via the internet. It could even be a secret addiction to pornography. Anything that secretly removes your emotional time and attention from your relationship with your partner is emotional infidelity.

When we talk about deception and betrayal it goes without saying we have to talk about pain, and the element that causes the most pain is lying. When someone you love deceives you by lying, the one thing you can't lose sight of is that they have made a conscious choice to deceive you; therefore they have made a conscious choice to hurt you. What makes lying so disturbing is that no matter how hard you may try to rationalize your partner's behavior (and believe me, we are all guilty of that, it's the most natural thing in the world to do) it just doesn't make sense. Why would the one person you love, who tells you he loves you, deliberately set out to deceive you? Lying takes away your ability to know what is real any more – you may find it hard not only to believe what he says but also to believe in yourself.

There are different types of lie – lies that involve what is said, and those that involve what isn't said. What is said are blatant denials of what is happening. They often go something like this: "There's no way I'm having an affair"; "I would never do anything to hurt you"; "I'd leave before I did anything like that". Lying by omission is where the lies are harder to define because they are unspoken. They always involve neglecting to tell you important information that would affect how you dealt with a particular situation. It's a bit like assuming that what you don't know won't hurt you. For example, your partner may neglect to tell you they have an anger problem, or a drug, drink or serious financial problem. Being aware of any of these problems would allow you to choose whether you want a relationship with this person. Lying by omission doesn't allow you that choice.

I'm sure Elin Nordegren never wanted to be the wife of a serial cheater, but that's what she ended up as. Tiger Woods didn't have one affair, he had dozens; in fact he had so many he checked himself into an expensive clinic as a sex addict.

You see, in the 21st century serial cheaters no longer have to be seen as dishonest or deceitful – they're apparently suffering from an illness beyond their control: sex addiction.

But at what point does a man go from being a cheater to a sex addict? How many women does he have to sleep with? Surely Warren Beatty, Hugh Hefner or Mick Jagger would be mortified to think they have been suffering from an illness they haven't known about for most of their adult lives. But Hugh Hefner has recently stated he thinks sex addiction is just a "cop-out excuse for adultery", adding, "most people who cheat do it because they think they can get away with it."

Opinion is divided within the medical fraternity as to whether sex addiction really exists. Many medical professionals argue that the condition is really obsessive-compulsive behavior and not really an addiction, a way out for people who want lots of sex to excuse their behavior. But that hasn't stopped a therapy industry with expensive clinics and 12-step programs from springing up and thriving.

Certainly citing sex addiction as the reason for his affairs has not seen Tiger Woods' image improve; the notion that Tiger was ill, and that was why he was cheating on his wife, is in many people's eyes ridiculous. We'll watch this space with interest.

How we react when we are confronted with the fact that our partner has betrayed us can say a lot about us as people. But men and women, gay, straight or bi react in very different ways. Men tend to leave a relationship abruptly; the majority of women will stay.

Take former US Secretary of State Hillary Clinton. She may be one of the most powerful women in the world but she's also a prime example of a woman who stays. With all the resources available to her – education, money, social standing and power – she has chosen to remain in a marriage with a husband whose philandering ways were splashed across the world's media for years. In her autobiography, Hillary wrote, "I am committed to my marriage", which I don't doubt for a moment. However, more importantly, one would have to ask her: "Is Bill?" Taking into account the rumors of Bill Clinton's previous dalliances with Paula Jones and Gennifer Flowers, among others, Hillary's answer would have to be "No".

The best barometer for the future is always the past. It doesn't matter that it's now over a decade since the Monica Lewinsky scandal, nor does it matter that Bill and Hillary are now well into their sixties – the fact is that like so many other women who choose to stay, Hillary will live with elements of stress as long as she remains with Bill.

If you stay, you've got to live with it every day; you've got to sleep with it; you are reminded of it every day. Here's the truth: it's way easier to leave an abusive relationship than it is to stay. You don't have to check your partner's wallet or their jacket pocket; you don't have to try to get their cell phone while they are asleep and see what messages are on it. You don't have to worry about what they're up to when they are half an hour late coming home. That takes up so much of your energy, time and personal well-being – and when you're abusive partner's gone, that's all gone.

Sandra Bullock always said her husband Jesse James was the love of her life, the man she couldn't bear to be parted from – until she found out he'd been cheating on her, that is. Sandra decided the stress of staying with Jesse would outweigh the pain of leaving him. So she left.

As women we've been culturally conditioned to be the nurturers, the caregivers, and the glue in our relationships. But the reason we suffer the way we do in situations such as betrayal is so simple: we allow ourselves to be treated this way. We allow it to happen, and so often we allow it to continue. Basically we send a message to our partners that says "it's OK to treat us this way'. You're yelling and screaming, ranting and raving, or your staying silent, will do nothing in the long term unless you change your behavior. You set your relationship up how you want it to be.

So here we are in the 21st century. Well, that's what I have to keep reminding myself. You would too if you spent a few days working in my office with me. I listen to literally thousands of stories about sex, lies and betrayal, and I find that not one person is any better equipped than the next to deal with it all. And you know what — that doesn't surprise me. What does surprise me is that we think we should be able to deal with it.

Back in the old days before disposable nappies, when a woman had a baby she had to be shown how to fold and put on a cloth nappy; there wasn't some primal instinct that kicked in, there was a nurse. The same goes for relationships. I suppose our earliest introduction to and memories of relationships come from our parents, and that in itself is a scary thought, although it's not their fault. How could our mothers teach us, or their mothers teach them, if they didn't know how to maintain a relationship with their husband without, in many cases, sacrificing their relationship with themselves? Back then mothers didn't teach their daughters how to be feminine, independent, assertive and powerful because they didn't know they could be all these things. Instead they taught them to be nurturers and homemakers, rather than the protectors and providers many women are today.

In my mother's day most women were full-time mothers and took pride in that role. Most women with children today don't have that luxury as they are juggling motherhood, a career and trying to maintain a successful relationship. All of these responsibilities require skills our mothers never had to use. They couldn't teach us what they didn't know.

You might have been lucky enough at high school to have received some sex education. However, sex education is a very different beast to relationship education. What sex education doesn't do is teach you what to look for in a mate, how to relate on an intimate and emotional level and, more importantly, how to be a good partner. If we had never been taught to read and write, how would we know what to do? Of course the answer is that we would be illiterate, and you could say many of us are still illiterate in the relationship sense.

What we must do is learn how to communicate on an intimate and emotional level, but how can we, when even today as a society we are still embarrassed to talk about sex and intimacy. This never ceases to amaze me – we all got here by the act of sex. If we can do it, why can't we talk about it? Back in my office I listen to couples who don't know how to communicate what they truly want, feel or need out of fear that their partner won't understand, won't listen or won't care. So many of them lie, cheat and deceive because they figure it's easier. Is it any wonder that so many of us at some stage of our lives find ourselves in a mess?

I'm afraid the news isn't very encouraging when we go looking for help from the professionals. Textbook theories might work in a perfect world, but we are far from having that. Research tells us that two-thirds of couples attending counseling for relationship issues will be worse off, or no better off, a year down the track. So if theorizing isn't the answer, what needs to be done?

After reading many books written by psychologists I'm struck by the fact that they always give examples of affairs where the betrayer has admitted his guilt. In all the thousands of clients I've dealt with, I can't remember one example of a husband volunteering that information. Even in the face of irrefutable evidence many will continue to deny it, until the evidence is so overwhelming it becomes impossible to keep up the deception. In some cases they never stop denying, no matter how much evidence is thrown at them. In most instances these betrayers have deceived their partners more than once. So that's where textbook psychologists and I part ways, and that is why this book has had to be written – for the thousands of women out there suffering at the hands of serial deceivers.

When my clients read a book in which the betrayer volunteers a confession and shows his remorse, they can't relate to it. In fact they feel even more disillusioned. They think that there must be something terribly wrong with them, or their husbands would do the same thing. So my way is to lay it out there warts and all, dispel the myths surrounding infidelity and give good honest, practical advice on how it really is, not how we think it is.

Often our success in life is defined by how successful our relationships are. Take the couple who have been married for 37 years – they must be successful, right? Not necessarily. Many of my clients are in longstanding marriages but have suffered more than one betrayal. The marriage only seems good from the outside looking in. Take the person who's been married more than once – like me. Surely there must be something wrong with me, right? Wrong. Let me tell you something I know for sure: it's a darn sight harder to stay in a destructive relationship and live with doubt and stress on a daily basis than it is to leave. It all comes down to what you think you're worth, and having the courage and strength to stand up for yourself in an abusive marriage shows that you respect yourself. Among my clients I've lost count of the number of marriages of over 30 years' duration in which the woman has stayed in an abusive relationship and has lost all self-respect. And remember, not all abuse is physical; it can also be through control or betrayal.

This book is all about you and looking after you. I'm not interested in anyone else. I'm not going to spend time trying to fix the men or women in your life. That isn't my intention and it shouldn't be yours. You're not responsible for them. You're only responsible for yourself – and it's you who matters.

This book is meant for people of all ages and all sexual orientations; after all, anyone can experience the pain of infidelity at any age. While you can't have a full understanding of infidelity unless you have experienced it, to have some understanding of the subject and be forewarned is better than being totally ignorant about it, as most of us are. My hope is that you will gain sufficient knowledge to alert you to the potential for emotional and financial heartache, because in 99 per cent of the cases I deal with financial infidelity goes hand in hand with emotional infidelity.

This book should help you understand what I absolutely know. You may be uncomfortable reading some of the chapters, for example, the chapter on how to have an affair, but it's there for a reason – to illustrate that the perfect affair doesn't exist. I'll show you how to spot a cheat at 1000 paces, what you need to know to move through betrayal if you're right in the thick of it, and how to prevent it happening again.

There have been times during the writing of this book when I've stopped and thought, "Am I being too tough?" and wondered whether I should have taken a softer approach. And yet the truth is, the reason so many of us has found ourselves dealing with infidelity or betrayal is because the soft approach hasn't worked. When you consider that the vast majority of my clients are between 30 and 60 years of age, there is no excuse for not knowing right from wrong, or a healthy choice from a destructive one. More often than not the solution lies with the person on the receiving end of infidelity and not the perpetrator. So, if this book seems hard going at times I'm not going to apologize. As we know, the truth often hurts, and the book has been written with the very best of intentions. I hope and trust that once you have read this book, you will never need to read another book on infidelity.

Finally, you might assume that because I work in a field that deals with the negative side of human nature I must have somehow been scarred by it, that I must be a deeply cynical person. Well, if you thought that you would be wrong. If you learn from its bitter lessons, then infidelity can bring you something good: it can give you another chance to find real love. I know this because it happened to me.

CHAPTER 1

Dispelling the Myths of Infidelity

Have you ever listened to the conversation at a dinner party when the subject is someone you all know is having an affair? Speculation is rife about why it's happened, and you may hear gems such as: "Poor old Bill's probably not getting it at home, so what's he meant to do?" or "Oh, he's probably just having a midlife crisis," or "It's no big deal, all guys play around," or even, "It's probably that new girl he employed; he told me she was hot. She probably came on to him – it's not his fault."

All these comments are based on a number of myths that surround the subject of infidelity. Let me explain how infidelity really works.

If you can smell smoke you can bet there's been a fire. How often have you been to the letterbox to collect the mail without giving it a second thought? Every day? Then one day there's an envelope addressed to you and you don't recognize the handwriting. You quickly scan the letter to see who sent it, and find it's unsigned. As you start to read the neatly written words, your heart begins to pound and you find yourself frozen to the spot. What you read is numbing and you actually have difficulty registering the words, so you reread the letter, at the same time wondering who could do such a dreadful thing – who could send a letter saying your husband is having an affair and they thought you should know about it? What type of vindictive, hurtful person could write such words? By now your mind is racing. You look at the writing again, you study the envelope, and all the time you're thinking, "This is wrong, why is it addressed to me?"

I'll tell you why it's addressed to you. It's because it's meant for you. Think about it. How often do your happily married friends get letters like this? Never, I bet. This letter is part of a carefully constructed plan. Usually these plans are masterminded by a lover who has either been jilted or is trying to bring the relationship to a head, a jealous work colleague, or someone who has simply had enough of living with the knowledge that your husband is having it off with someone behind your back.

In the greater scheme of things, and you won't realize this while your heart is pounding in your ears, this person has actually done you a favor. What was hidden from you may have remained hidden for much longer had it not been brought into the open like this.

I think I have to say at this point that if something like this should ever happen to you and you can honestly say on the deepest intuitive level that you have never had any previous concerns, then maybe, just maybe, it's come to the wrong address. But if there's one tiny doubt in your mind then it has most likely come to the right address.

Take Claire, for example. When she phoned me she was hardly able to speak, but after a few attempts through the tears she finally told me that a magazine (you know the kind) had come through the post, addressed to her, and of all days it was her twenty-second wedding anniversary. The sender had written captions on Post-it notes and placed them next to certain photos. The captions read: "Your husband likes to do this to me."

As the conversation continued, Claire said that if she were honest there were many times throughout her marriage when her husband's behavior would change and he would become vague and elusive about times and events. Like so many women with a busy lifestyle and family commitments it was easier for Claire to ignore many of these signs.

> *I knew Barry was lying when he had these memory lapses and couldn't remember who he had lunch with or what hotel he'd stayed at. He was a lousy liar but I could never prove it. For a time I even convinced myself that Barry was suffering from some kind of dementia. I just needed to believe that the man I had shared 22 years of my life with, and had two children with, wasn't a lying cheat – there was always a story, always an answer. Even when the pieces came together and I had seen things with my own eyes I still doubted myself. Like the time he told me he was going to work at the weekend; I drove to his work and all through the car park, both front and back – and his car wasn't there. Then I called his direct line and it rang and went to voicemail so I tried his mobile but that was turned off. When Barry finally came home complaining he'd had a hell of a day I told him I had called round with some lunch and his car wasn't there. He looked at me and said, "What do you mean my car wasn't there? You couldn't have looked very hard – I've been there all day." That was his story and he was sticking to it. If I continued to challenge him I'd only get the guilt trip – how hard he worked for the kids and me, how lucky I was to have such a great lifestyle... I pretty much knew the drill and could recite it word for word. Yet I felt sick to my stomach as I looked at the magazine in my hand, and I couldn't imagine who would send it to me. What does this woman have that I don't?*

In actual fact this magazine was meant for Barry. The person who sent it knew the only way to get to him was through Claire.

Let's look at Claire's story in order to dispel some of the myths of infidelity.

Myth 1

'The other woman must be prettier than me.'

Claire couldn't imagine who would do such a thing, nor could she imagine what kind of woman had enticed her husband away – was she beautiful, slim, young and sexy? It's a question that has been asked of me thousands of times and the answer is surprisingly difficult for my clients to accept. From time to time your husband might make comments about some luscious creature he's seen on TV and you imagine he wouldn't say no, given half a chance. But in reality the chances are that the luscious creature wouldn't be in the slightest bit interested in him. This is what many women find hard to believe.

My clients are forever telling me how good-looking their husbands are. In other words, they truly believe other women are going to find them irresistible as well, but I have yet to find one of my clients' husbands appealing, and I have literally seen hundreds of photographs of men of all shapes, sizes and ages.

What women have to realize is that men are looking for something quite different. Remember, your husband isn't looking for a wife (he's already got one), he's looking for sex and I'm afraid to say that the package doesn't have to be that flash.

In essence, it just has to be easy and available. Married men who play are the easiest prey to snare and that's the absolute truth.

And to answer Claire's question — "What is she like?" — the answer is she's a flat-chested, 5 foot 2 inch, mousy brown-haired size-14 insurance clerk. On the other hand Claire is a 5 foot 8 inch, vivacious, attractive, size-12, 40-something financial planning consultant.

In nine out of ten cases this is exactly how it is — the "other woman" isn't younger, prettier, slimmer and smarter than you; she's just ready, willing and available.

Myth 2

'He's having a midlife crisis.'

This myth is illustrated in what Sarah said to me:

You can't tell me that any man in his right mind is going to walk out on a 37-year marriage on Christmas Day when his daughter is flying in from England the next day. Is he having some sort of midlife crisis?

I'm always skeptical when I hear the words "midlife crisis" as I have clients with husbands whose ages range from 20-80, so I'm not sure where "midlife" starts. In Sarah's case, as we delved deeper into her 37-year marriage it became clear that she had proof of Greg's numerous infidelities dating back to the very early years of their marriage. However, this was the first time he'd left her and she felt she needed to give his behavior a label – "midlife crisis". She could use this label to explain her husband's behavior in terms of the commonly held belief that men of a certain age are prone to infidelity, when in fact he had always behaved this way.

What women in Sarah's position need to be aware of is that what Greg did in leaving isn't particularly uncommon for men in their sixties. His children were all married and living overseas. He and Sarah were very well off financially and he held considerable power in the business world so in his eyes he'd done his duty by his family. In his head he'd left the marriage many years ago.

Sarah, for her part, like many women, had deeply ingrained beliefs about relationships, handed down through the centuries. Whenever trouble arose, Sarah reacted as the nurturer and caregiver, doing everything in her power to right the wrongs, and sending a very clear message to her husband that she would always be there, fixing things when they went wrong. In behaving this way women set the ground rules for the marriage.

Sarah was shocked when Greg left, although his behavior showed he was a prime candidate for this. The key points here are that "you set your relationship up the way you want it to be", so you can't ask, "Why has this happened to me?" You have to take responsibility for your part. Greg very clearly showed Sarah that he was a philanderer, and a serial philanderer at that, but we all have choices and with those choices comes an element of risk. Sarah's choice was to stay in her marriage. So, to answer Sarah's question, "No, it's not a midlife crisis – it's a crisis that's been waiting to happen."

Myth 3

'He's not getting it at home.'

It is often assumed that when a man embarks on an affair it is because his wife isn't coming up with the goods. Well, have I got news for you!

This is the story of three attractive, intelligent women: Beverley, Marie and Sue. They all came to me with the same problem: they were living in sexless marriages. Collectively the total amount of celibate time was 43 years and it wasn't for want of trying on their part, contrary to what most people might think.

Combined, their marriages equated to 82 years. Looking at it one way, they had been without sex for almost half their married lives. I know it's hard to imagine anyone would stay in relationships like this, but I find this situation to be increasingly common. Beverley is married to Tom, the managing director of a large and successful company.

> *Tom moved out of our matrimonial bed because he said he didn't want to disturb me when he came home late from work functions — and that was 14 years ago... I always thought it was a weak excuse because I have always been a heavy sleeper.*

Marie is married to Frank, a barrister.

> *Frank moved out of our bed saying that I disrupted his sleep with all my tossing and turning — and that was 16 years ago. What I found strange was that once Frank was*

in bed he was so exhausted he fell asleep instantly and it would have taken an earthquake of 10 on the Richter scale to wake him.

Sue is married to Trevor, who owns a large dental practice.

Trevor told me he felt guilty because he couldn't get an erection so he thought it best to move into the spare room in the hope that loneliness might make something grow harder – that was 13 years ago and according to Trevor it never did.

In Beverley's case we discovered the reason Tom was staying out so late wasn't because of long business meetings or work-related functions but because he'd discovered a lust for very young women and spent his time in massage parlors.

No one could have kept Frank awake, not even the restless Marie, because he was actually living dual lives. He was in a full-blown relationship with a work colleague with whom he had set up home.

Trevor didn't have erectile problems until a few years ago but then he discovered Viagra. When Sue found four packs of Viagra in his car the game was up and Trevor was found to have been visiting a family friend every morning on his way to work.

Sex isn't everything in a marriage but if you talk to the person who isn't getting it then you realize how important it is. The intimacy you get from a physical relationship is what sets it apart from a friendship. If you have a good physical relationship in your marriage it only rates 15 per cent on the scale of importance, but if there's no sex in the relationship it rates 95 per cent on the scale of importance. That level of importance can only have a negative impact on the relationship overall. I cannot stress this enough and I'm going to keep on saying it until you get it – you set your relationship up the way you want it to be.

All three of these women have been clients of mine for a long time, and all three have received absolute proof of their husbands' infidelity. Yet all three have stayed in lonely, sexless marriages, trying at every opportunity to rekindle the fire, and all the time their husbands have been lying and deceiving them. The way in which each has set up her marriage isn't based on a single event or a single action. Not only does each of these women have a dysfunctional relationship with her husband, but they all have dysfunctional relationships with themselves as well. The relationships within their marriages can only exist if they are nurtured and actively encouraged by a lifestyle that supports them. All of these women have, through their actions in condoning their husbands' behavior, helped shape the lives they are living right now. In fact, the way in which they have set up their marriages and chosen to react to inappropriate behavior from their husbands could only have had one result.

At this point let me make myself perfectly clear, because I can hear you all screaming: "Condone it? You've got to be kidding!" No doubt some of you will have said something to your husband or partner along the lines of: "You do this one more time and it's over, you're out of here. How can you keep doing this to me? I'm going to tell your boss, your mother, your friends and your little floozy that you're a lying cheating bastard." Yeah, yeah, yeah – he's heard it all before, and what do you keep doing? You cook his meals, you wash his clothes, you tidy the house and you keep the homes fires burning. You've set your relationship up so that your man has the best of both worlds. Why should he change?

Do you see what I'm saying? Do you get it now? However, the next time you hear the old myth that someone is having an affair because he's not getting it at home, think of Beverley, Marie and Sue and don't assume it's because the woman doesn't want it.

Myth 4

'Men play around more than women.'

When Jim confided in me that he suspected his wife Yvonne was up to something and hired one of my investigators to watch her on her days off, we didn't really expect anything too out of the ordinary. We couldn't have been more wrong. Yvonne was followed to an inner-city supermarket car park, but that's as far as she got: shopping for food was the last thing on her mind. My operative watched as a man approached her, got into her car and then was driven back to her house. An hour later Yvonne drove the man back to the supermarket and dropped him off, but she didn't leave straightaway; instead she waited in the car park again.

The real surprise came two minutes later, when another man approached Yvonne's car and got in. Again Yvonne and the man drove off, back to her house. Another hour went by, and lo and behold, Yvonne and her friend emerged and drove back to the same supermarket car park. My investigator, increasingly goggle-eyed, watched Yvonne repeat the same operation two more times in succession that day.

We reported back to Yvonne's husband and told him what we'd seen. I remember he was shocked but didn't seem that surprised, and he asked us to watch Yvonne again on her next day off. We did just that and of course exactly the same thing happened: Yvonne met a series of men in the same supermarket car park, then drove them home and returned them within the hour. It turns out Yvonne had a profile on an adult dating site where she was looking for discreet sex; the only thing was, it wasn't just for pleasure – Yvonne was charging for it. Her husband was distraught, but he told me he had originally met Yvonne on an adult dating site, and they had very quickly established a relationship.

When it comes to playing around, women can be far more calculating than men. Yvonne was an opportunist who used her feminine wiles to get not just sexual pleasure, but money as well.

Jeff's wife Kate is very typical of the female mindset, in that if she thinks she can bring her love interest into the home, and then make no mistake, that is exactly what she will do – with you there. The difference is that men will take their lovers home, but nine times out of ten you won't be there.

> *If I told you that my wife goes swimming at the local pool and she returns home with her swimsuit and towel wet but they don't smell of chlorine, what would you think? She's not the type to have an affair.*

Let's answer Jeffs question logically. The pool she swims at is chlorinated, and since Kate's swimsuit and towel don't smell of chlorine she hasn't been swimming there. Jeffs following statement is very common amongst men: "Kate's not the type to have an affair." Well, what type of woman is she and what type is it that has affairs? I'll let Jeff explain the rest.

> *My wife Kate is a keen swimmer but I've never really enjoyed the water, although I've always wanted our children to learn. So when Kate started to take the children to evening classes I was happy for her to indulge her love of the water while teaching the kids to swim. After a few weeks Kate began to talk about a guy she'd met, called Colin, who also took his children to the pool and how he and his wife Jill, who often collected them, seemed a nice couple and perhaps we should invite them over for a barbecue one Sunday.*
>
> *It seemed a good idea and we all got along well with the kids having a great time. Slowly Colin and Jill became a fixture in our lives and joined our circle of friends, and six months later we all went on holiday together. The only thing we didn't have in common with our respective spouses was swimming, as both Jill and I hated it, so Kate and Colin would take the kids to the water at every opportunity.*
>
> *Then about 18 months ago Kate and Colin decided they needed more competition, so as well as the Tuesday night swim sessions with the kids they started training together for triathlons, which meant Thursday training at the local pool and Sunday morning cycling and running. We continued to socialize and spend considerable time together until one night Kate returned from one of those Thursday night training swims, and as she undressed and emptied her sports bag the one thing missing was the*

unmistakable smell of chlorine. I said nothing at the time but each Thursday after training I waited for that most unmistakable of smells but never did it enter my senses again.

We found the reason for the lack of chlorine when we followed Kate to a hotel across town where she was greeted by the reception staff like a long-standing customer. She paid the bill in cash and went up to a room, and within five minutes Colin had arrived in a taxi and gone straight up in the lift to join her. Further enquiries showed she had booked the room in her maiden name, and the reason she was so wellknown was that she'd booked the same room for a further 12 months.

So, Kate did what a lot of women do. Women are drawn by a strong emotional connection as well as a strong physical connection. In Kate's case this was demonstrated by the fact that she brought Colin and Jill into their circle of friends in order to spend more time with Colin than would have been possible under the circumstances of a normal affair. As a result of her planning, Kate and Colin managed to deceive their partners by using friendship and their children as a cover. When women like Kate are finally uncovered their downfall doesn't come from their husbands' intuition — Jeff had been oblivious to the ongoing emotional deception and certainly hadn't noticed a change in Kate's behavior. What he had noticed was a physical change, with the lack of the smell of chlorine.

So, in trying to dispel the myth that men play around more than women, you need to understand how it became established. You only have to switch on the news or open a newspaper and there it is — another rich, famous and powerful man having an affair. How often do you see a woman of similar standing shown in this position? Very rarely, I would say. With the exception of the late Diana, Princess of Wales, I can't think of many. Throughout history how many powerful women (and there have been many) have been shown to be adulterers? Yet from Henry VIII to John F. Kennedy and in recent times Tiger Woods, rich, famous and powerful men have often been shown to have marital affairs. The difference is that these affairs have been condoned and often trivialized, or even depicted as a man's birthright. Women, on the other hand, are castigated and called harlots, whores and sluts, and in some countries are put to death for those same marital infidelities.

In modern Western society there are just as many women betraying as men — the reason we don't hear or read about it is that women plan their infidelities and men don't. Generally women deal with love, sex, friendship and partnership on a very different level from men. This doesn't mean their needs are any different, however, and that is where men make the mistake of assuming their wives wouldn't play around. Women use this way of thinking to their advantage.

A second advantage for the woman who wants to play is that men are less intuitive by a country mile and just don't pick up on the small things. This, in combination with a good dollop of male arrogance (nine out of ten men, when asked if they thought their wives would cheat on them, said no), gives a woman plenty of scope to carry on an extramarital affair with little chance of being found out.

My experiences show that women plan for the possibility of being caught out, while men don't consider this or more importantly don't care. When I have asked men, "Did you ever consider you might get caught?" the usual reply has been, "No, I'll deal with it if it happens."

I don't want to appear unsympathetic but this book is all about reality and in many cases men are the masters of their own demise. Just as women who stay with their philandering husbands send a message out that says it's OK to be treated in this way, men also need to be aware of what's happening around them and be conscious of the little things. By appearing uninterested you only make it easier for the woman with betrayal on her mind to carry it through.

Myth 5

'There's got to be something wrong with her or he wouldn't stray.'

In Myth 1 it is the wife asking the question about the other woman ("Is she younger, sexier, etc.?") whereas in this myth it is the wife who is under scrutiny. This myth is based on the perception that the betrayed must be imperfect or lacking in some way, such as being less attractive, less intelligent, dowdy or dull, when in reality this isn't true. The fact is, it has nothing to do with the woman and everything to do with the man who is cheating. To be convinced of this you only have to look at the late Princess Diana, Jennifer Aniston, Sienna Miller, Nicole Kidman and Halle Berry. These women have been recognized as some of the world's most beautiful and desirable and yet their men, who would be hard-pressed to find anyone of equal caliber, and who you would therefore think would be more than content, have still betrayed them.

So, you tell me what's wrong with these women that they

have been betrayed? These are all beautiful, intelligent, vivacious and talented women. What other qualities could they possibly possess to prevent this happening to them? Can you see the picture emerging, that it isn't the betrayed with the problem but the betrayer?

What I find interesting in my work is that 95 per cent of my clients are attractive, intelligent, professional women who never thought they would be betrayed. They thought, like the rest of you, that it only happened to the dull and dowdy. The reason the truth hits so hard is partly because they are intelligent and they can't believe they chose a philanderer as a partner – they thought they were smarter than that. Because they do take pride in how they look and present themselves , the biggest blow comes when they eventually find that their husband's love interest is as I described in Myth 1 – someone who isn't as attractive, who isn't smarter, and is not even younger than they are.

Tiger Woods provides a good example of what a man is prepared to risk for sex. He really did have it all – wealth, fame, love – but he risked it all for shallow flings with a series of low-rent cocktail hostesses and bar girls. You could say these women sure as hell weren't a patch on his wife Elin Nordegren when it came to the looks department. And despite all the high-profile sex clinics and expensive PR, only time will tell whether Tiger's behavior towards women and sex will change.

An example from my files is a woman called Debbie. She's typical of my clients in that she is an attractive, intelligent career woman in her early forties. To fulfill her business commitments Debbie travels abroad one week in each month.

I'm sure my husband is up to something. He's been acting

strangely of late and every time I come home from overseas he seems really uptight. God, this is so hard and I hope you tell me I'm wrong, but I've got this feeling and it won't go away. On my last trip I came home unexpectedly and found his screwed-up mobile phone bill in the kitchen waste bin, and when I examined it there was this one number that jumped out at me because he had called it six times a day, every day for the time I was away. So I called it and I think I recognized the voice but I can't be sure. It sounded like the woman he used to go out with before me. I've seen her and she is absolutely ghastly – I would never have thought she was his type ... I'm probably wrong because I'm sure Steve told me that she'd just got married recently. Anyway, I guess what I'm wanting is to have him watched the next time I'm away.

Steve had gone to play golf, and we could see him on the veranda of the clubhouse with his playing partners. His car was at the rear of the car park out of sight of the clubhouse, and as we watched a battered old BMW pulled into a space next to it. Within minutes Steve appeared pulling his golf cart and bag, and he began loading his car. He then went to the passenger window of the BMW and leaned in. Then he got into his own car and both vehicles left the car park. They drove to a nearby reserve where she got out of her car and into his. The first thing we noticed was that there was no sign of a wedding ring. Now it takes a lot to shock me, but shocked I was because this woman, apart from her height and hair coloring, was the complete opposite of Debbie. Her hair looked as if it hadn't been washed for days and she looked as though she had been poured into her clothes; they were so tight there was bulging flesh everywhere. But judging by their actions Steve didn't seem to mind at all. Now Steve is what you might call affluent, so the second surprise was when they dined at Burger King, which led me to think that Steve didn't have to blow the budget on this woman.

Myth 6

'He would never bring anyone into the matrimonial home.'

There are two forms of this insidious behavior and both are extremely common. The first form is where the act of infidelity is taking place outside the matrimonial home but the husband or wife finds ways in which to introduce their betraying partner into their circle of friends or have them invited to parties and social functions. Kate, described above in Myth 4, is an example of this. Josh is another.

After Celine finally confronted Josh about his affair with his work colleague Georgina, she was shocked when she realized how many times Georgina had been to her home for barbecues and dinner parties over the previous two years. Then there had been the many company functions Josh had organized, which Georgina had more often than not attended on her own as her partner, according to Josh, was always away on business.

Only after the evidence became compelling did Josh finally admit that his stolen moments with Georgina during the week hadn't been enough. The only way in which they could see each other more often was for Georgina to be invited into his home, with the cover of her partner, which offered a false sense of security to Celine.

The second and most blatant form of this behavior is when the betrayer takes his lover back to the matrimonial bed. This is the hardest thing for any woman to accept since not only is she herself not considering infidelity, but the house is her home and the last place she would want to defile. The first thing a woman needs to do is to stop thinking along her own moral lines and consider that if her partner is having an affair then he isn't playing by any rules but his own, and that means anything is possible – including sex with another woman in the matrimonial bed.

There are a number of reasons men take their lovers home. Some men will avoid spending a dollar unless they have to, and there is also no paper trail to worry about, as there would be in the case of a hotel or an illicit weekend away. And for some men there is the perverse excitement of thumbing their nose at their wife by having sex in the home.

> *I went away on business for three days and came home earlier than expected. Although the house was empty it looked as though Des hadn't been out since I left. The place was a mess and when I went into the bedroom I noticed the bed was unmade and there was a pile of crumpled tissues on the bedside table. When I picked them up a used condom fell to the floor. As I bent down to pick the condom up Des walked in, and when he noticed me dangling the spent condom in my hand his expression resembled that of a stunned mullet. I asked him to explain and he said he'd masturbated that morning, to which I replied, "Since when have you become a hygiene freak? Did you not want your hand to catch anything?" There was no answer, and in my eyes there was no explanation;*

Des had committed the greatest sin of all, crapping in his own nest.

It should be noted, too, that if a woman is trying to take a man away from his wife, and the man is dragging his feet, his mistress may try to hasten the demise of his marriage by leaving a trail of clues to be detected by his wife. This can be as subtle as the smell of an unfamiliar perfume left in a lover's car, or a 'mislaid' item of clothing, make-up or jewelery. Whatever, it's all done on purpose, a nasty way of trying to bring things to a head.

Myth 7

'She's just someone he can talk to but it's not sexual.'

When a client calls me their intuition is telling them that although this is what he is saying they can't quite accept that it's true. They try to rationalize the situation by starting the conversation with these words it's their way of justifying and minimizing the facts. It's like when people use the expression "I slept with so and so" when in actual fact they are having sex with that person – the word "sleeping" makes it sound more acceptable.

Let's be honest here – these words aren't coming from the client but from their partner. This is what he has said to her, and he is doing exactly what she is doing when she is talking to me – minimizing and justifying.

In all my experience of clients using these or similar

words, the fact of the matter is that the betrayers never get to eat, drink or sleep together because they're too busy stealing moments during the day to have sex.

While Emma was out shopping she saw her husband sitting at an outside cafe table with a young woman she recognized from his work.

> *I watched them for about 15 minutes and their conversation was quite animated as they leaned in to one another across the table. When Justin came home I waited for him to raise the subject but he spoke about everything else except his coffee with the woman from work. I became agitated and in the end said a friend of mine had seen him having coffee with a woman. I asked him why he hadn't told me about it when he had discussed everything else about his day. At first he said he'd forgotten, and then he changed his mind, saying it was unimportant but she was getting married soon and they'd been discussing her wedding plans over coffee. This had me boiling for a number of reasons, firstly because this cafe was miles from their office, but more importantly because when we decided to marry, Justin had left all the planning to me – all he had to do was turn up and he couldn't even get that right because he was late. So I said to him, "Since when have you been employed as a wedding planner?" But instead of an answer he just said they found each other easy to talk to, and, "Hey, nothing's going on if that's what you're getting at." At that point he stormed out and I was left to sit and consider what I had seen and his reaction to my questions. Over the next few days I thought I'd managed to justify everything to myself but my intuition was saying the opposite so I picked up the phone and*

discovered there was no wedding because there was no fiancé, no boyfriend, no man in sight but my husband, her lover.

Myth 8

'Where does he find the time to fit infidelity into his busy day?'

Again there is an assumption here that infidelity, betrayal – call it what you like – is about love, romance and intimacy when in fact it's about sex – plain and simple. So when this question is asked think about how long it takes to have a sandwich and coffee and then consider the time from penetration to ejaculation. A quick interlude is hardly a grand romance and getting to know you and meeting family and friends doesn't come into the picture, so an hour would be a luxury and 15 minutes is fine and plenty of time to get the deed done.

Remember: motels offer daily and hourly rates; parks and reserves are free; cars are cramped but mobile; boats are private and secluded, and there is always home. Most married people who are playing with another married person have to choose these snatched moments during the day to avoid alerting their spouses, so don't be surprised if they're home in the evening because the deed is being done by day.

Another form of betrayal is the variety that you pay for, where she supplies the room and all the necessities to have some fun. Times can vary from 15 minutes to an hour and can be booked ahead of time or just taken pot luck.

Some time ago when I was watching a client's husband, who was suspected of having an affair, I parked across the road from his office outside a beauty therapist's establishment. There was a sandwich board outside on the street offering facials, manicures, therapeutic massage and, down at the very bottom, stress relief. I must have sat there for most of the morning before I realized I hadn't seen one woman go in or out of this establishment. However, over lunchtime I noticed trade became quite brisk, with men in everything from business suits to shorts entering and leaving the premises. Then I noticed my client's husband enter, and he re-emerged an hour later looking extremely relaxed and relieved of stress. He then went on, bought a sandwich and went back to work.

As I sat there I decided to time the men coming in and out and found they were spending between 15 minutes and an hour inside, so to confirm my suspicions I sent one of my male investigators in to enquire about their services. He was told 15 minutes for a hand job, 30 minutes for oral sex and an hour for full intercourse. So while my client thought her husband was munching away on a chicken sandwich he was actually ... I'll leave it up to your imagination.

Myth 9

'It wasn't his fault-she threw herself at him and seduced him.'

In Myth 7 ("She's just someone he can talk to but it's not sexual"), I said that my clients' intuition was telling them that although this was what he was saying they couldn't quite accept it as the truth. This myth is similar, in that the words are there to mislead you into rationalizing, justifying and minimizing the facts.

Take Grant, for example, who, after being caught, went to great lengths to explain to his wife that he didn't even fancy the woman he'd just had sex with. When she tried to justify his actions to me I pointed out in my usual diplomatic manner that if she was prepared to believe this garbage then there was little point in trying to convince her otherwise. However, she decided to listen as I explained the facts as they really are. To get an erection there has to be some sort of attraction, so I asked her if they were both fully clothed when sex took place – to which she replied, "Well, no, he told me they were naked."

"So what you're saying to me is that their clothes just fell off. Did she have a gun?"

"What do you mean, did she have a gun?"

"Well, firstly he didn't fancy her but got an erection and then, having not fancied her and got an erection, he took his clothes off, so I have to assume that after all of that and then to have intercourse she must have threatened to shoot him in the balls, because if she didn't, there is no excuse."

In conclusion – the fear of being shot in the balls would make any self-respecting erection disappear at an amazing rate of knots. The reality is that he fancied her, he wanted her and he had her – and that is the only explanation for what he did.

Myth 10

'All men play around, don't they?'

This question infuriates me because clients use it to justify their partners' behavior. If all men play around, why should they feel bad about it? This statement is a cop-out which comes from a woman who is too afraid to face the truth; it is easier to accept the devil you know than the devil you don't by convincing yourself that any other man is going to be the same as the one you have. Therefore, what's the point in thinking she could make a difference?

Sometimes when I hear this question I know exactly why it's being asked and what has brought it about. The client has irrefutable proof of her husband's infidelity, in fact so much proof that he can't do anything but admit to the affair. However, he has immediately put Plan B into effect – minimization. I can hear him now: "Look, I don't know why you're making such a big deal about this. Everyone does it. I'm not unique. I can give you thousands of cases. And anyway, it's over now and it won't happen again." Acceptance of this type of behavior is born out of fear and women who believe this are very wrong indeed.

Of course not all men play around; there are many men of integrity out there and the sooner women realize this the better.

Myth 11

'This will shock you.'

All my clients think their story is unique and that I will be shocked. All cases are different in that the protagonists vary in the degree of emotional entanglement and hurt they feel, but throughout all the thousands of cases I have dealt with there are common threads and behavioral patterns that link them all. Because infidelity is so devastating to them and they have an emotional connection, clients expect me to be shocked at their story. However, I liken it to an undertaker who deals with death daily – when you telephone him to tell him a relative of yours has died you don't expect him to be shocked. So why should they expect it from me? The reason is that we can talk more freely about death than infidelity or betrayal because infidelity and betrayal are about sex, and that is something most people find difficult to discuss at the best of times. For me (like the undertaker) there are new casualties every day so I have pretty much seen and heard it all.

Myth 12

'Julia, there must be danger in your job.'

Most people assume there must be an element of danger in my work and I suppose to a degree there is, but not the sort you may think. The only danger I face is stress, and that goes with the territory. Infidelity is such an emotionally-charged topic that there will always be a handful of people you're never going to please no matter what you do. Usually these people are the ones who have left a situation for far too long and then want a quick fix. It's incredible how some clients have been seduced out of hundreds of thousands of dollars, have been emotionally betrayed for years, and have spent thousands of dollars on lawyers, yet if I don't come up with the goods immediately all their problems become my fault. I had one such client not so long ago. The call went something like this:

> Oh Julia, I can't believe I've been so stupid. How could I have been so blind? Everybody has been telling me for years that he's been ripping me off, but why would someone do that? What makes a person do such things? I'm such a mess. I don't know what to do. He's left me and I think he's with another woman, but why would he do this to me? He's only just got back from four months overseas and I never questioned him about what he does when he's away. He doesn't even have to work because I do that. I don't think he's having sex with this woman, but I need to know who she is.

After an hour or so I had calmed her down enough to tell her she should see her doctor just to get herself something to help her through the initial stages. I don't advocate the taking of drugs, but sometimes a situation is just too overwhelming to handle without help and that was certainly the case for this woman. I also gave her the name of a relationship law specialist because I felt that was going to be more effective at the stage she was at than my services, considering he had already left and had been fleecing her financially for years. Who the other woman was at this time was immaterial, and we could always follow up on that at a later date if she felt the need. She went on to tell me that for the last 20 years she had basically kept this man – bought him cars, paid for overseas trips that he would take on his own – yet she would never question what he was doing , and she would have no contact with him at all while he was away.

I know what you're thinking. You're thinking I must be making this up because no one could be that stupid. Well, I'm not, and this is not an isolated case. This woman is a success in business and very intelligent, but in emotional terms she is weak and vulnerable. As the conversation continued I had to start popping vitamins to help keep the stress levels down because this story went from bad to worse.

She had found emails from a number of women he'd met overseas, which spoke of their passion, lust and feelings for this man, and yet she still believed he was being faithful to her despite telling me that the one thing in the world he wanted to be was a porn star!

She said she couldn't go on without finding out who the current woman was, and she asked if I could find out for her. She had an address where she thought her ex-partner was living. I told her we would find out, and then carried out some surveillance at the property, but lo and behold she turned up wanting to play detective. As far as we are concerned this is an absolute no-go area – you either leave us to do the job or you do it yourself. The last thing my investigators need is an emotionally charged person getting in the way.

No matter what I said she wouldn't listen, and you didn't have to be Einstein to work out why this man had behaved the way he had. He'd had all the opportunity in the world and she knew it, but because I hadn't come up with the answers she wanted to hear I was useless. Even if I had she would have wanted more, so I will guess that I wasn't the first investigator she'd called, and my commiserations are with the next.

Another frustration is clients who confront their husband or partner with every snippet of information they've obtained during the ongoing surveillance. This alerts him to be careful, which makes our job so much harder and longer and in some cases can completely blow any chance of catching him. There are times when I feel that some clients subconsciously sabotage the investigation because they can't confront the reality.

If you are going to hire a private investigator, you need to have thought through exactly what you are going to do with the information and how you are going to deal with the "worst case scenario". I find this is where clients fall down. They expect to be proven wrong, and when the opposite occurs they aren't prepared to deal with it.

Key points

- The lover doesn't have to be younger, prettier, sexier or slimmer than you. No, they just have to be up for it, and let's face it — there's no easier prey than a married man looking for sex.
- Forget using midlife crisis as an excuse for infidelity because if he's that kind of guy and he's got a pulse then he's a risk.

- "He's having an affair because he's not getting it at home, right?" Wrong.
- "Men play around more than women." Wrong. Women just don't get caught so often.
- "There's got to be something wrong with her for him to stray." Yeah, right I so tell me what excuse did Tom Cruise have with Nicole Kidman? Jude Law with Sienna Miller? Jennifer Aniston with Brad Pitt? Hell, if something was wrong with these women what chance is there for the rest of us?
- "He would never bring anyone back to the matrimonial home." You want to bet? When the small head is leading the big head all reasoning goes out the window. Men just don't have the same emotional attachment to the family home as women do.
- "She's just someone he can talk to but it's not sexual." Yeah I and pigs can fly.
- "Where does he find the time to fit infidelity into his busy day?" Anytime he can find between 15 and 60 minutes because this is about sex, period.
- "It wasn't his fault she threw herself at him and seduced him." He knows right from wrong and he made a conscious decision to betray. Don't fall for the "It just happened" story, because how often do your clothes fall off of their own accord?
- "All men play around, don't they?" No!

CHAPTER 2

Julia's story: Part 1

A woman has got to love a bad man once or twice in her life to be thankful for a good one."

Marjorie Kinnan Rawlings

It's taken me four marriages and half a lifetime to know the real truth in those words. I've had my share of bad men and tough times, but believe me when I say it doesn't have to be like that. Nowadays I am married to the man of my dreams; I am an internationally published author, TV and radio personality and a successful businesswoman who runs an international private investigation company.

Getting there wasn't easy, but the good things never are.

Back when I was 15 you could have written down what I knew about boys and human nature on the back of a postage stamp. The truth was, at 15 I wasn't interested in boys – my love was directed elsewhere, at a rather rotund 13-year-old strawberry blonde chestnut mare. I spent every moment I could with her; we were inseparable. The only problem was every time I rode her home I had to pass a house that was littered with old cars and boys tinkering with them. So it was inevitable, I suppose, that the girl with the strawberry blonde hair atop the strawberry blonde mare would create a diversion. And that's how it started.

I didn't know how old he was, the one who eventually caught my eye, but he seemed to be the alpha male of the pack: good-looking and mature. He was 25. He asked me out to a party. I asked my parents if that was OK; they said "No", he wasn't the kind of company they wanted me to keep.

My dad was born in 1904, a true Victorian Englishman. He was a scholar, a writer, poet, painter and musician, and 50 when I was born. He loved hunting and fishing and he introduced me to archery by the time I was 10; by 12 I was a dab hand with a .22 rifle.

My mother was of Scottish descent, creative, gentle and the most amazing homemaker. I always felt there was so much more she should have done – she was not meant for life in New Zealand. She was 39 when I was born.

We lived in a semi-rural street in west Auckland, in New Zealand. The boy from the scruffy family down the road was definitely most unsuitable for my parents' only daughter. But in true teenage fashion, I was dead set on going to that party with him. Looking back, I know my parents allowed me to go only because of my insistence. I am sure they were trying to juggle doing the right thing with allowing me a little freedom, but I can see now how hard it must have been for them to let me go.

My mother made me a pretty blue dress for the big night, and at the party I sat at a table drinking what I thought was orange juice. I later found out it had been liberally spiked with vodka. I still remember the head rush I got when I tried to stand up and immediately passed out. Apart from the odd glass of sherry at home with my parents, I had never really drunk alcohol before that night. The next morning I woke up alone in the boy's bedroom with blood on the sheets. I immediately thought, "How embarrassing; I've got my period."

The boy came into the room and told me that he'd phoned my parents the night before to say that I had become ill and would stay at his parents' home. I knew my parents would be very angry but at that moment I still did not realize what had happened because I was so sick I was throwing up. Nowadays they call what happened to me date rape.

Six weeks later I missed my period. I knew enough to know this was really serious. Going to the family doctor was out of the question so in my naivety I booked in with another doctor in the same practice using my middle name. No one would pick that up, I thought. When the doctor came out to reception to get the file for his next patient he looked over at me and said something to the nurse. He then called the next patient and the nurse motioned to me to come to the desk. I was quite pleased when she gave me back the money I had paid, and thought, "What a nice man for not charging me." I later found out that all maternity care was free.

When it was my turn, there was no internal examination; the doctor just looked at me and knew that this 15-year-old girl was pregnant. I knew my parents would be terribly upset and I didn't have the courage to tell them face to face – there was a phone box across the road from the surgery and from there I told my mother I was pregnant. It was the first and last time in my life I heard my mother cry. But she wasn't upset about what other people might think, she was crying for me and what she knew I would have to face.

In those days a girl in my situation had two options: to go away to a home for unwed mothers to have their baby and then have it adopted out, or to keep the baby and endure the shame of being labeled a "bad girl", someone who had disgraced the family name. As far as I was concerned, from the moment I knew I was pregnant I was keeping my baby come hell or high water.

The next problem was how to tell my dad, and it took

nearly four months for the truth to come out – by that time I couldn't hide it any longer as the obvious was beginning to show. I'll never forget the night my mother said, "Hartley, Julia has something to tell you." I looked at her and said "What?" as you do when you feel your life is about to end. Dad looked at me and said, "Well then, what is it?" And at last, in despair and relief, I told him. There was a terribly long silence as we all sat there waiting for someone to speak. Finally my father asked who the father was. "Well, my girl, you had better tell him to come and see me because he will have to marry you." Dad later told me he gave him an ultimatum: marry me or be charged with carnal knowledge of a minor.

Of course, under the law I wasn't allowed to get married until I turned 16, so it was agreed by my father and the man who had taken my virginity that on my 16th birthday I would marry him – a man who, if I'm honest, I didn't know, let alone love.

That agreement was also the only reason the authorities would let me keep my baby: an underage girl of 15 was simply not allowed to keep a child. I remember so clearly back then that no one talked TO me – only ABOUT me. I don't think I was ever asked about any of the decisions that were being made about me, and my life.

I felt I must have been such a disappointment to my parents; they were both academics and my brother excelled at school too, but alas I did not. From the day I started at five I couldn't stand it, and that never changed until the day I left at 14 years old. My parents had known it was pointless keeping me in school, so the following year, and before I turned 15, I was working full-time in a shoe store. I loved it, although it was never going to satisfy me long term unless I owned the shoe store. But that all changed when I got pregnant.

I've always found it hard to believe those stories you hear about women who have babies without knowing they were pregnant. The reason I went to the doctor in the first place was because I felt so strange, without really understanding why. My life changed dramatically from then on. The only thing about pregnancy that I enjoyed was the fact that for the first time in my life I had boobs. It must have looked ridiculous when I was pregnant – me lying in my single bed in my pink bedroom, surrounded by dolls and my riding gear and the smell of olive oil. My mother, God bless her, made sure that every evening after I put on my special nightgown I rubbed olive oil into my stomach to avoid stretch marks (the experts tell us it doesn't work, but I don't own a stretch mark).

I could not have survived without my parents and they did the best they knew how. I had the very best maternity undergarments money could buy, but as to how the baby would be born or, more importantly, where it would come out, no one told me this. These things weren't discussed. I never went to an antenatal class, and as for the pains of labor, they were never talked about either, so when I went into labor six weeks early it caused a bit of panic. I was told I was going to have a premature baby – well what did that mean? It would have two heads? My fiancé took me to the hospital, where they started performing bizarre procedures on me. First of all they shaved off my pubic hair, and then they came towards me with a rubber hose and told me it was going up my bottom. The next thing I knew I was being filled up with water; apparently this was called an enema. I thought they were trying to drown my baby.

I had been there for about 15 hours when they said there were complications that they weren't equipped to deal with, so I would have to be packed into an ambulance and taken to

National Women's Hospital. It was another six hours lying in the dark on my own before my daughter was born. All the while I could hear screams coming down the corridor from women in the agony of giving birth. I remember the doctor coming in to check on me, and asking him how I would know when the baby was coming. And he said, "Believe me, my dear, you will know." How right he was.

Because of my age and the premature birth, as I was wheeled into the delivery suite I was asked by one of the doctors if I had any objection to some medical students coming in to observe. Any woman will tell you that at that moment when the baby is about to be born, you don't care if the whole world is watching, so I agreed. No one ever forgets the first moment they see their baby, and I was no different. My new daughter was a little fat beauty, but I only saw her for a few seconds before she was taken away. The next second, a document and a pen were shoved into my hand and I was asked to sign away my baby for adoption. I threw the pen across the room and refused.

It was three days before I was allowed down to the premature baby ward to see my daughter again. Imagine my horror when I was presented with a child that was not mine. I told the nurses they'd given me the wrong baby, and they tried to tell me they hadn't. Luckily after a check they started to believe me and went in search of my baby. They found she had been mistakenly placed in a ward for babies that were destined for adoption.

After the birth I was wheeled away to a ward where on first glance I thought there'd been some mistake: I wasn't supposed to be with the old folk, was I? All these women seemed so old, but no, they were just normal mothers – I was the odd one, a kid with pigtails and big pink ribbons.

A few months later I thought all the drama was behind me, although the truth was, of course, that it was just about to begin. My daughter was born in December 1969, and I married her father the following February. In just a month's time I was pregnant again, this time with twins! I should have taken those pills they offered me while I was in hospital, but because my 15-year-old self felt fine I declined the offer – no one explained to me that the pills were contraceptives.

By this time, my single bed had been replaced with a double and my husband had moved into my parent s' house and into my pink bedroom while we waited for our new home to be built. I never gave the house much thought and found it hard to get excited about it, which was probably because there was so much else going on. It was a nice house, with three bedrooms and a double basement, but at the time all I was concerned about was my constant throwing up. The weeks went by and at three months pregnant I looked six months.

From the outset I couldn't understand how different this pregnancy was from the first – and the movement I was feeling had me thinking. Apparently my doctor already thought it was a multiple pregnancy but once again I was kept in the dark. I was still throwing up all day and every day, and in my seventh month my doctor decided I needed an x-ray (there were no ultrasounds in those days). I had to lie on my back with a huge strap across my stomach which was pulled tight in order to flatten my belly. And while I held my breath they took the x-ray. As usual, nothing was said, and home I went.

Two weeks later I visited my doctor for a check-up and he was muttering away, seeming quite pleased with his diagnosis. Just as I was about to leave he turned to me and said, "Do you know, my dear, you're having twins?" I looked at him and then, just as you've seen in the movies, I felt myself slowly slipping to the floor. Eight hours later I was in labor seven weeks early.

This time I felt like an old pro – it was straight to National Women's Hospital. And when I saw that rubber hose coming my way again I told them exactly what they could do with it! Thank God the labor was quick this time – I couldn't have endured what I had been through the first time. But pain relief? What did that mean? All I got was a few puffs of gas – that was it. I delivered one twin in the hospital corridor on the way to the delivery suite. Twenty minutes later, the second baby was out.

So there I was, 16 years old, married, with three babies under a year old. At that time, I often thought about something my school principal had said to me just a year earlier: "Julia Moore, you'll never amount to much." Who could blame her? I bet there were a lot of people who thought that about me – but you know something? I was brought up never to think of myself as a loser – in fact I can remember feeling very proud of my babies and of myself for surviving what I'd been through.

Around that time I met another young mother just a few years older than me, let's call her Sue. Sue had just had a baby daughter too. We had a lot in common – it was great to have someone to confide in and we became close friends. Our husbands became great friends too; you could say it was a cozy little foursome. Sue would visit me during the day as it was more difficult for me to get out with my brood. We were still living in my parents' house, and it was my mother who was the first to notice that she always arrived around lunchtime, right about when my husband came home. Initially, of course, I thought nothing of it, but I do remember having a strange uneasy feeling – I know now that the feeling was my intuition, but at 17 I had no idea what intuition was. Back then I always just dismissed it.

Until the night all four of us were invited to a party. All night I sat with an empty glass while Sue's glass was constantly topped up with wine by my attentive husband. Something felt bad, and it was going to get a whole lot worse.

A few weeks later, my parents announced they were going away on holiday. As a married mother, and now 17, they thought I was old enough to be left to take charge of the house and children. So, after they had left, I decided it was time to throw my first dinner party. I invited Sue and her husband, and we all seemed to be enjoying ourselves until Sue announced that she felt unwell and needed to lie down for a while. Had I known what was going to happen I would have made sure she stayed down! She went into our bedroom and lay on the bed. A few minutes later my husband said he needed to put something away in the garage while I made the coffee. Sue's husband and I made our way into the lounge with our drinks and began watching television.

Twenty minutes later I heard a nagging, familiar noise, though it took some time before I realized just what it was. It was the squeaking of our bed. I can remember turning to look at Sue's husband; he had the same ghastly, disbelieving expression on his face that I did, and we both stood up together and walked to the bedroom. He pleaded with me not to go in, but I simply had to open that door. It was like being hit with a brick – there was my husband lying on my bed straddled by a naked Sue right in the throes of passion.

What did I do? I can remember being physically sick from the shock; the rest was a blur. I think I blacked out. How I tended to my babies I'll never know but I suppose I must have stayed in that marriage for another two hellish years as my husband pretty much did as he wished. We moved into our new house and my parents advised me to stay with him for the sake of the kids; it was simply what was done back then. And every night I got into bed with someone who'd betrayed me.

Eventually, though, I just couldn't keep up the pretence. After many nights staring at the back of my husband's sleeping head, of agonizing over what to do, I told him that I simply couldn't live like this anymore. He left for work that morning and never entered the house again.

I was left with my children, and questions. How could my husband have done what he did? Why did he do it? It wasn't for the want of sex, that's for sure. Would it have made a difference if I had dyed my hair black and grown it long like Sue's? Was there something wrong with me, is that why he'd strayed? Of course there wasn't – I know now that it wasn't about me – but back then I had many lessons still to learn.

CHAPTER 3

Intuition

How can something you can't even see be so powerful? Intuition is an acute subconscious connection to your environment. In contrast to every other species in nature, humans can choose to ignore intuitive signals and often don't even recognize them. We disregard our intuition unless we can find a logical explanation for it. Even when our intuitive feelings are strong and clear, we often seek other options rather than trust ourselves. The amount of emotional energy we use looking for a safe explanation could be put to better use evaluating the information we have.

Intuition shows itself in a variety of ways: gut feelings; nagging feelings and thoughts; suspicion; doubt, hunches and apprehension. These feelings can linger for weeks, months and even years. Intuition should never be ignored. If you've opted to disregard it up to now but the signals are still persistent, you may just have overlooked the signs of betrayal your intuition is telling you are there.

The signs

Let's get physical

Out of the blue your man says it's time to lose a bit of weight, tone up the old body and generally get in shape. Any sudden changes in behavior are key signs. For example, Sue's husband hadn't been a slob by any means, but he enjoyed his food and apart from playing golf he did little to keep fit. Then he decided to join a gym – but not one close to home, where he and Sue could work out together – it was on the other side of town, and even then it was some distance from his office. When Sue enquired why he'd joined a gym so far from home he trotted out the excuse that it was cheaper and they ran programs for people who were just starting to get in shape again.

And so his new regime started, but when we investigated we found his workout regime was a little different to the one he'd told Sue about. Yes, he did go to the gym early each morning, but on some days, and especially on a Saturday (Sunday was his day of rest) he would join his lover at her home – where he would still get extremely physical in the horizontal position.

So what was it that alerted Sue to his indiscretion? Well, first of all it was the obvious, the sudden change in behavior. But second and most important, it was that a gym with such a cheap membership scheme could afford the most expensive French soap for their showers!

Sex, too much or not enough

When someone withdraws from you sexually or wants more sex, or starts suggesting positions you've never used before, then again we're looking at sudden changes in behavior.

Sarah and David had been married for 28 years when he began to ask her to try new ways and positions. When Sarah mentioned this, David became defensive and said they'd done these things before and she'd just forgotten. Sarah was sure she would have remembered these acts and positions, as they were very different from their normal lovemaking. Of course, this change in behavior alerted her so she began a little detective work of her own. Sifting through David's credit card statements Sarah began to find strange companies listed. When she showed these to me I instinctively knew none of them would have listings in the telephone directory, as they were fronts for massage parlors – a little surveillance work proved the point.

When the opposite occurs and someone withdraws from you it's important to remember there are different degrees of withdrawal, from a slowing of your normal sexual activity to a complete stop. The slowing down of sexual activity can often be the sign of a lustful or emotional attachment elsewhere, and a complete stop is often the sign of a fantasy being fulfilled. Anyone will have difficulty competing with this. Another sign is when your partner withdraws to the spare room, citing sleep disturbance as an excuse.

Increased sexual activity initiated by your partner is often designed to lull you into a false sense of security. This happened to Jackie, who couldn't get over Damien's new zest for making love. When she asked him if he was seeing someone else he told her that if he had any more sex he'd be dead. Jackie wasn't put off the scent for long and employed us to check him out – and so it was shown that his actions spoke louder than his words, as his sexual activity at home was more than matched by his sexual activity elsewhere.

Breastfeeding the mobile phone

Secrecy is one of the biggest giveaways that someone is betraying you. There's nothing wrong with retaining one's own privacy but excessive secrecy in a marriage is another thing altogether. Watch how someone behaves with their mobile phone. Do they:

- Keep it close to them at all times?

- Take it into the bathroom with them?
- Take it with them when they put the rubbish out?
- Constantly look at their phone (a giveaway for text messages)?
- Start walking away out of earshot if it rings when you are close by?
- Leave it in the car or switched off and occasionally check for messages?

The key here is that when you have nothing to hide you hide nothing. When your partner is hiding something from you, you'll notice that the phone bill, bank statements and credit card statements conveniently end up at work, and in fact nothing comes home at all. Recently, while clearing the company post office box one of my investigators noticed a man nearby clearing his box – when the man opened his mobile phone account he tore up the list of calls into very small pieces, threw these into the waste bin, then wrote out a check and posted it off with the bill. Think about it – when you have nothing to hide you hide nothing.

So when you ask to see these records, whether it's for phone or credit card, your request can cause a huge problem. You may be told they've been thrown away or that they'll be brought home but they never seem to materialize. Don't accept these excuses – records are kept for seven years and a call to the phone or Credit Card Company will elicit them within a few days.

Mobile phone bills

The mobile phone bill is a sure-fire giveaway if someone

is having an affair. The sheer number of calls should be all the proof you need. I say "should be" because in my experience it never is. Don't be swayed by excuses such as: "She's a work colleague. What do you want me to do, send smoke signals?" No matter how hard he tries to talk his way out of it there is no way out. A mobile phone bill is tangible evidence, and that's why the phone account is the first thing that's removed once an affair begins. Getting your hands on an account is always a bonus.

Should you manage to find the account, you may notice a certain phone number has been called eight times in one day, then ten the next, five the next and so on, so you decide to call it and a female answers.

Then you need to look at the times and lengths of the calls and compare them with the times and lengths of calls he makes to you. I bet there is a huge discrepancy in favor of the calls made to her.

Now you need to look and see if he calls you straight after one of those calls. You may see a pattern emerging – when he calls her then you it's usually to see what you 're up to and to reassure himself everything is fine at home. If his phone is off for any length of time during the day you may see she gets the first call when it's back on, and then you again. This is his way of continually reassuring himself that you are oblivious to his deception.

As you go through the account you'll see this kind of pattern repeated a number of times. It's easy to figure it out. First ask the obvious, and that is: have you seen this sort of pattern before? Think about this. If you have a platonic male friend, do you call him between five and ten times a day? Do you phone him first thing in the morning and last thing at night? Do you make very short calls (i.e. leave messages) or send text messages on the weekend? Somehow I don't think so, because we don't even call our best girlfriend that many times day. But if you're in lust, well, that's different, and to hear their voice is the next best thing to seeing them.

Betrayers are switching to the use of prepaid phones to conduct their affairs. This is because there are no phone bills to contend with, so the betrayer feels he has less chance of getting caught. If you've noticed certain numbers that were being dialed on his normal phone have stopped appearing on his bill, this can be a sign that he's using a prepaid mobile. You need to check the credit card or eftpos statements from around the time that these numbers stopped appearing, to see if there's a purchase of a phone or of top-up cards, as this is often the way in which these phones are replenished with minutes. Most people buy these top-up cards in quite large denominations and use a credit card or similar to purchase them. Also check for patterns of cash withdrawals that can't be substantiated by a receipt.

It's likely the prepaid phone will never be seen in your home – it will be hidden either at work or in the car. Good places to check are under the driver's and passengers' car seats, or if the car has a folddown rear seat, lift the seat squab and check under there. The spare tire compartment is another hiding place, as is the compartment that holds the car jack and tools. If you can gain access to his briefcase then search that too, although in these circumstances this is likely to be kept locked.

Once again, remember the saying: "If you have nothing to hide you hide nothing."

Receipts, bank statements and credit card bills

Have you ever been really excited by a receipt you found while innocently emptying your husband's trouser pockets? For example, a receipt from a jewelery store for a gold bracelet when it's your birthday in a few days' time? Have you ever had that sinking feeling as your birthday comes and goes with no sign of a gold bracelet? Instead you get a card with the promise of a holiday – but you've had those promises before and the holidays have never materialized. If you ask him to explain the receipt he jumps down your throat and accuses you of snooping. Then he tells you that you've spoilt the surprise so now you can forget it. A reaction like that is guilt at being caught out deceiving you.

I had a client who phoned me because she had found such a receipt, and she was furious, not because her husband had bought some gold earrings, but because he had bought some inexpensive ones that she would never wear. She knew full well they weren't meant for her since her husband was very well aware of her expensive tastes. As you can see, the humble receipt can tell many stories.

The same applies to credit card bills. How many times have you tried to figure out some odd amounts from companies you can find no record of? These aren't usually for huge amounts; often they are for just over $100, and there isn't usually any pattern – unless, of course, you bring them to your husband's attention. Then the only pattern you'll notice is that they never appear again.

These companies are the fronts for massage parlors. All massage parlors have confidential credit card facilities so the item looks benign on your credit card bill. Look for company names with the word "Holdings" in the title then try doing a company search and you'll find there will be no street address, no phone number listing. In many cases no such company exists.

Bank statements can be another give-away, as one client found when she was looking for an amount she had paid for car repairs and discovered a cash withdrawal at the same time each week. She discovered this was child support for a child she knew nothing about — a child who had been fathered by her husband during their marriage.

Too many details

When someone wants to deceive you a technique that is often used is to give too many details. When someone is telling the truth they don't feel the need to go into great detail. For example, if they were late meeting you for lunch they would simply say they were sorry for being late. But someone who is lying needs to justify the lie to themselves. Their reasoning probably sounds plausible to you but it doesn't to them, so they keep on talking, trying to add additional support to their story.

Take, for example, the guy who phoned his wife and started to describe the plane trip he'd just taken, every turbulent bump, what he'd eaten and who sat next to him. The only problem was that he hadn't taken the plane trip at all, and his wife was receiving his call in the same hotel foyer as he was making it from. She told me later that if she hadn't seen him with her own eyes she would have believed his story, although it was a little over the top — he was a regular flyer and normally wouldn't have described such a mundane flight in detail.

Getting defensive

You'll notice when you ask what used to be a simple question, such as "When will you be home?" he becomes defensive, and if you challenge him he may become verbally aggressive. The surfacing of this behavior is usually a sign that guilt is lurking somewhere. His response becomes a verbal assault, such as: "I'm sick of being questioned. I can't do anything right – no matter what I do it's not good enough. You always think I'm doing something. Why don't you ring everyone and ask them what I'm doing? I'm trying to do what you want." So now it's turned onto you and you're probably feeling really bad for asking a simple question. Answers like this reek of guilt; the easiest way for a betrayer to camouflage the lies is to turn the situation around and attack the innocent party.

Overly attentive

Remember what I said before? That sudden changes in behavior are tell-tale signs? So, if you've lived with a guy who's never taken much notice of what you wear and what you do, then all of a sudden he starts complimenting you on how you look, or decides it's time you had a holiday on your own away from the kids because you work so hard and deserve the break, beware – especially if he is displaying any of the other signs we've talked about.

Take Tricia's husband, for example. He did just that. He suggested she needed a break and because things were so busy for him at work she should go on her own to New York for three weeks. That's when she telephoned me, because it was so out of character – he'd never been so considerate in their

16 years of marriage. We only had to watch for the first week because he never went home after that and couldn't be contacted by phone at home. Wouldn't you just know it – the phone lines were out for two weeks? Our enquiries showed no faults were found and the phone was off the hook the whole time.

Talking about a particular person too much

Talking about someone doesn't necessarily involve making positive comments about them. Sometimes a man will come home from work, as Roy did, and start to make derogatory comments about a new female colleague. Roy would tell Natalie how useless his new colleague was, and he would also throw in comments about how she was no oil painting, knowing full well that in the short term making comments such as these would put Natalie at ease. The problem for Roy came when Natalie began to notice how many times this woman's name was mentioned.

When someone is attracted to a person, that person is always in their thoughts and to talk about them, even in an unflattering way, is an excuse to keep that person in their mind. When Roy first started behaving this way Natalie thought nothing of it, but after a while she started to notice that not a day went by without his mentioning this woman. When Natalie had to go out of town for a night she had Roy watched. True to form, Roy had his little oil painting over to watch some naughty movies.

Another way men try to cover their tracks is by talking about the new female they have met and her husband or boyfriend, or the fact that she's soon to be married. All these scenarios are little smokescreens. They think the simple mention of a man in the same breath as the woman will keep their wife off the scent. Peter told Viv that his PA, Sally, was finally getting married in six months' time and was impossible to work with because she was so preoccupied with her wedding arrangements. Peter even went as far as to invite Sally and her fiancé round for dinner. However, at the last minute the fiancé wasn't feeling well and couldn't make it. Peter suggested Sally come anyway. I remember Viv telling me how uncomfortable she felt that night. She said watching the pair of them was like intruding on a private relationship. We later found out there was no fiancé or wedding, and that Peter and Sally had been having an affair for 18 months.

Hang-up calls and strange messages from the unknown

I think not! I'm always intrigued as to how women can find logical reasons to justify strange hang-up calls in the middle of the night or cards, letters, magazines and newspaper cuttings when they come through the post. These are all very obvious signs of betrayal, which usually come from a dumped lover although in some cases they're from someone who knows what's going on and wants to alert the wife. However, they are usually from a woman scorned.

The one fundamental thing women who have affairs with married men forget is that the man they're involved with is lying to his wife. So why does the other woman think he's telling her the truth? When she finally realizes that what she thought was the truth is actually a lie (and he's never going to leave his wife) that's when it's more likely you'll receive unexplained mail or anonymous calls.

The husband of one of my clients got in first. He knew there was a very real possibility that something along these lines could happen, so he told his wife a crazed woman was stalking him. The only thing that didn't stack up was that he never reported this alleged stalking to the police. Of course, the reason he hadn't reported it was obvious; the woman in question was far from crazed and the only mistake she'd made was to become involved with a double-crossing, lying cheat.

The business trip

I wonder how many of you are familiar with this. When you're married to a professional man and he has to go away on business, does he:

- Only find out about it the day before he's going to leave?
- Not know how long he'll be away and not know where he's staying?

Because if he's keeping you so much in the dark that you might as well be a mushroom, then he's also ensuring the chances of you finding him out are virtually nil.

Once again to figure this out is easy. If you're planning a trip away do you know where you're staying, when you're leaving or how long you'll be away? Of course you do. And so does he.

Let's have a look at a couple of cases we have investigated recently to show you just what lengths some people will go to in order to use the business trip as a cover for infidelity.

John, a successful surgeon, was in his third marriage to a

professional woman whom he had met and had an affair with while still married to his second wife. (This is a huge warning sign: "If he does it with you the chances are he will do it to you." It pays to keep that thought in mind.) So, in effect, my client had first-hand knowledge about how her husband would conduct an affair. Since we are all creatures of habit I asked her to cast her mind back to those days, because he was probably doing the same thing now. Lo and behold, we were right. He flew to a city thousands of miles away, booked into a hotel, instructed the staff to take a message should anyone ring, then hopped on the first available flight back home – where he drove straight from the airport to his lover's house. He then telephoned the hotel, retrieved his messages and called his wife as arranged. Fortunately for our client, "the best barometer for the future is the past," and this prompted her to take a trip to his hotel. When she arrived she was informed by the reception staff that her husband wasn't there, and he had instructed them to take messages.

Brian had started to go out of town on business. His trips were always unexpected but, as he explained to Shirley, it was due to some restructuring within the company that needed his personal attention. Once again one of these trips had come up and he would be away over Valentine's Day, the very day Shirley had arranged a special evening for them to enjoy. Shirley had a very uneasy feeling about this trip. Brian wasn't due back until two days after Valentine's Day, but on the day she couldn't get rid of a persistent doubt so she checked the time of the last flight from his destination. She waited at the airport and, sure enough, who walked through the automatic doors but Brian. She was just about to approach him when she saw a woman meet him, and she watched as they went out and got into the woman's car. She then followed them, and when they pulled up at a set of traffic lights she was directly behind them. She saw her husband turn and the color drain from his face as he recognized her.

Now you're probably wondering why these women are clients of mine, having caught out their husbands themselves. The answer is simple. Despite having irrefutable evidence they have done nothing with it, and they have employed me to find out if their husbands are still playing around.

Sex kit

Ever wondered why he's precious about you fossicking around in his car or the garage? Well, maybe it's because you could, quite by accident, stumble on his 'sex kit' as Joan did.

Even when Richard was out of town, Joan would never drive his car. She had no desire to because she considered her Audi far superior to his Porsche. But on this particular morning she had no choice. Her car had a flat tire and fixing it would make her late for work, so she hurriedly threw her things in the boot of Richard's car and took that. When Joan arrived at work she took her things from the boot and noticed the boot lining was pulled out of place. As she attempted to straighten it she noticed a small box like a cash tin sitting in the tire well. The box was locked so Joan searched Richard's key ring and found one that opened it. Inside were two packs of Viagra, four packs of condoms, some lubricant and a type of spermicidal gel. Joan was literally frozen to the spot and her mind went into overdrive. Was this the reason Richard was so paranoid about her going anywhere near his car? It was the most logical explanation. She decided to count the condoms and the Viagra, put them all back where she had found them and say nothing for the time being.

When Joan got home that evening she went through the garage with a fine-tooth comb and found another stash. This time it was in an old sports bag shoved behind some shelving. According to Joan, she and Richard had never discussed the need for him to take Viagra. Her finding it was very disturbing, as it showed Richard had a secret life.

Viagra

When Viagra was developed it was hailed as a wonder drug, the savior to a man's manhood and the solution to relationships that had lost their oomph!

As always, let me throw a spanner in the works by telling you how I see the effects of Viagra through my clients' eyes. Because Viagra is aimed at men, women are often excluded from the discussion and the decision-making process, which is no surprise. Men are good at having sex but not good at talking about it, especially with the one person who is going to be affected the most — their wife.

Usually when a woman has to make a decision regarding her sex life she will discuss it first with her partner. However, this isn't what happens with Viagra. In fact, the pattern that has emerged during my investigations into infidelity is that the man doesn't discuss the situation with his wife, but simply obtains Viagra from a doctor, men's clinic or the internet. He then uses it for his own pleasure outside his marriage. In these cases the only time the wife finds out is if she accidentally stumbles across it, as Joan did.

There are the odd few who tell their wives after they've obtained the drug and use one in four tablets for the wife – the rest are used elsewhere. Again this only comes to the wife's attention when she realizes there is very little improvement in her sex life yet her husband seems unconcerned, which causes her to look deeper and discover what's happening to the tablets.

The moral of this story is that Viagra gives men who are prone to straying the ability to continue into their dotage.

It also doesn't surprise me that the makers of Viagra have recently abandoned attempts to use the blue pill on women. For years I've been saying it's foolish to assume that when a woman has an affair, it's just the same as when a man does. We all know men are physically driven – that's why the blue pill works so well for them. However, women are a tad more complex and need physical, emotional and intellectual stimulation. As a result, if these aspects are coming into play in an affair, there is a significantly higher level of risk to the marriage, and an increased chance she will leave for the other man.

Sleep disturbance

I bet you all think it's men who snore and make unimaginable noises at night, but apparently not. According to many men it's the night-time antics of their wives that drive them from the matrimonial bed and into the spare room – as Chrissie found out. Ben said Chrissie was too hot (her body temperature) so he moved out of their super-king-sized bed and into the poky little back room with a bed to match. As Chrissie explained to me, they'd had the bed custom made and four people could have comfortably slept in it without disturbing each other.

So what was the real reason Ben moved out? In my experience a lot of men will use an excuse like this to avoid having to face the truth, which is that they are having an affair. Men who move out of the bedroom have usually left their wives emotionally and this is their way of justifying what they're doing. There is no longer any intimacy and they don't sleep with or have sex with their wives. Women who accept this behavior, even if it's not what they want, are condoning it.

Pin numbers and passwords

Why do people have pin numbers and passwords? For protection and privacy, right? That's all well and good, but if you're in a monogamous relationship why would you have a pin number on your mobile phone that your partner doesn't know about, or a password on your computer at home that your partner never uses? I'll tell you why – "If you have nothing to hide you hide nothing."

Trish began to be concerned when her laptop computer malfunctioned and she needed to complete an assignment, so she switched on the computer in her husband's den. She was confronted with a request for a password. Not knowing what the password might be, she telephoned her husband and politely asked him what it was. She was taken aback when he flew into a rage, telling her he was far too busy to give it to her right then and she would have to wait until he arrived home from work.

Trish was so angry at his response she decided to try a number of possibilities – including his name, her name, the kids' names, the name of the dog and so on until she had exhausted every option she could think of. Finally, she keyed in the word "PASSWORD" and access was allowed. What she found was a complete email history of a relationship he was having with a business associate at the other end of the country. She printed it out and placed it in safekeeping for a rainy day. She then shut down the computer and waited for her husband to come home. When he finally arrived she told him she'd managed to have her assignment extended and she wouldn't require his precious password because her own computer would be fixed the next day.

When she went into his computer the next day in search of more information she found that everything she'd printed off the day before had been deleted – her husband was obviously concerned that he would have to give his wife the password and open himself up to being caught. However, his goose was already cooked.

Denials and Excuses

By now you may be asking how I can have such a one-eyed view of infidelity. However, anyone who believes I think men are the only betrayers is very wrong. As I've said before, not all betrayers are men and not all men betray. But what I also say with conviction is that you can't do a job like mine for as long as I have and keep hearing the same stories and seeing the same evidence and believe this is coincidental. That would be irresponsible, naive and stupid of me.

Ninety-nine per cent of the clients I see tell me they have experienced infidelity in their marriage or relationship more than once before coming to me. That shows me very clearly that once a philanderer always a philanderer. Let me point out that there is a difference between a repeat betrayer and someone who stuffs up once. If the one-time offender volunteers his indiscretion, actively seeks professional help of his own accord (in other words you don't have to tell him to get help), is willing to discuss your feelings and talk about your hurt, is patient with you, is prepared to be open and honest and is happy to keep you informed of where he is and what he's doing, then the chances are this person is genuinely sorry for his actions. Therefore, the likelihood of it happening again is heavily reduced. There are, however, never any guarantees.

With a repeat offender the only guarantee you have is that he will do it again. The repeat offender will deny, deny, deny to the death – even in the face of irrefutable evidence. In the Bill Clinton/Monica Lewinsky case, had there not been DNA, Bill would still be saying "I did not have sexual relations with that woman." This is very common behavior among serial betrayers and we encounter it all the time.

I had a client whose husband had a very distinctive car with a personalized number plate. We followed him as he picked up his girlfriend from work and then as they drove to a secluded beach where she performed oral sex on him while still in the car. We documented this and showed his wife, and there was absolutely no doubt that the man in the car was her husband.

However, when she confronted him with a verbal allegation, his first response was denial. When she told him she had hired a private investigator he still continued to deny that he had been in the vehicle. To this day he continues to deny he's done anything wrong. And even with so much compelling evidence my client still clings to the possibility that her husband may be innocent, based on the simple fact that he won't accept responsibility and admit any wrongdoing.

Another example of this is the way Hillary Clinton, an extremely intelligent woman, has coped with Bill's indiscretions. She only acknowledged the relationship between Monica Lewinsky and her husband because there was irrefutable DNA evidence and Bill publicly acknowledged it. The odds are stacked as high as Mount Everest in regard to Gennifer Flowers and Paula Jones but because Bill has never admitted to these indiscretions she publicly refuses to accept he is guilty, and she always will unless at some stage in the future he openly admits it. Constant denial is how serial betrayers get away with it time and time again; therefore there will always be a next time.

When a client calls for my help and I ask the usual question – "Has your partner ever had an affair before?" – the response is often, "Yes, I think so ... a few years ago I thought he was but I could never prove it." I'll bet these clients have had enough proof to know the truth, but the proof they are looking for and need is a confession from their partner. However, not one of my clients has been given a voluntary confession. This deny, deny, deny behavior is very male. Men hate to be wrong or to be seen to be doing wrong – and to be caught out is a sign of weakness. Women, on the other hand, when confronted about an affair may initially try to deny it, but more often than not a guilty woman will admit her guilt when pressed. That doesn't mean she won't do it again, it just means that women don't have the same degree of arrogance and ego that drives most male betrayers.

Key points

- Receipts, bank statements and credit card bills – when bank statements, credit card bills and mobile phone accounts are no longer sent to your home address but are redirected to his office you may have cause for concern.
- Too many details – when someone is telling the truth they don't feel the need to go into too much detail. For example, if someone is late meeting you for lunch they would usually just apologize for being late. But someone who is lying needs to justify the lie to themselves, so they go into far too much detail.
- Getting defensive – you'll notice that when you ask what used to be a simple question such as, "When will you be home?" he becomes defensive, and if you challenge him he can become verbally aggressive. This behavior is usually a sign that guilt is lurking somewhere, especially if he is displaying any of the other signs discussed.
- Overly attentive – remember what I said before? Sudden changes in behavior are the tell-tale signs. So, if you have lived with a guy who has never taken much notice of what you wear and what you do, and all of a sudden he starts complimenting you on your appearance, beware – especially if he is displaying any of the other signs we've talked about.
- Talking about a particular person too much – this doesn't have to be in a positive way; talking disparagingly about someone is meant to put you off the scent. Another tell-tale sign is talking about the new woman they've met and her husband or boyfriend, or the fact that she's soon to be married. If your partner is guilty of one of these patterns of

behavior, beware, because these are usually smokescreens to mask what is really going on.
- The business trip – when you're married to a business or professional man and he has to go away on business, does he only find out about it the day before he's going to leave? Does he not know how long he'll be away or where he's staying? Of course he knows all of these things – the reason he doesn't tell you is because he has something to hide.
- Sex kits (and other hidden secrets) – ever wondered why he's so precious about you fossicking in his car or the garage? Well maybe it's because you could accidentally stumble on his "sex kit", which often contains Viagra, lubricants and condoms. Other items like prepaid mobile phones may also be hidden in these areas.
- Sleep disturbance – when men move out of the matrimonial bed and use the excuse that you are disturbing their sleep, it's more often than not a way to avoid having to face the truth, which is that they are having an affair. Men who move out of the marital bed have usually left their wives emotionally and this is their way of justifying what they are doing.
- Pin numbers and passwords – when you find your access into phones and computers is blocked by passwords and pin numbers, this is a sign something is being hidden.
- Denials – there is a huge difference between a serial philanderer and the guy who stuffs up once. If he denies everything in the face of irrefutable proof, and continues to do so, this issue will never go away.

Stupid excuses

When someone is out to deceive you they will come up with the most ridiculous excuses imaginable, and if you were not so emotionally involved you would see these excuses for what they really are. But most women, even after hearing these stupid excuses, will find ways to justify them.

Evidence: You find a receipt from a strip club.
Excuse: "I just called in for a beer."
Truth: If you only want a beer and not to ogle naked women, go to a bar.
Evidence: Your husband is seen coming out of a massage parlor.
Excuse: "I needed some cigarettes and there was a car park right outside the door."
Truth: Gas stations and grocery stores sell cheaper cigarettes so why would you go to a massage parlor for cigarettes?
Evidence: Your husband comes home from a business trip and has porn magazines in his briefcase.
Excuse: "Someone left them in the rubbish bin in the hotel room and I didn't want anyone to think they were mine."
Truth: Who is going to care what you leave behind in a hotel room? Your husband is buying porn magazines.
Evidence: Your husband has been out of town on business, and when the telephone account comes in you see numerous calls made late at night and lasting for 30-60 seconds. They turn out to be to massage parlors and prostitutes. You ask why he's been ringing prostitutes.
Excuse: "Oh, just to hear someone say hello."
Truth: Why didn't he ring his wife?

Evidence: Your husband is seen out with someone he shouldn't be with.

Excuse: "I was just having coffee with her because she needs someone to talk to about problems in her marriage."

Truth: Since when did your husband become a marriage counselor? And he should have volunteered the information to you first.

Evidence: You find he's made calls every day on his mobile to another woman's mobile.

Excuse: "She's just a friend from work who I can really talk to."

Truth: Every day is excessive unless there is a legitimate reason such as work and he has volunteered the information rather than you having stumbled across it.

Evidence: Your girlfriend tells you your husband is having an affair.

Excuse: "You know she's jealous of us and she's trying to turn you against me."

Truth: He knows she knows and is afraid that soon you will know.

Evidence: You find evidence that your husband has visited a massage parlor while away on business.

Excuse: "It wasn't for me; Peter used her and I had to put it on my card in case his wife found out."

Truth: Let him know that you'll be asking Peter to reimburse you.

Evidence: You find a receipt for a substantial amount of money from a massage parlor in your husband's wallet, with his signature on it.

Excuse: "I was drunk and don't remember anything. I must have fallen asleep."

Truth: They don't charge you for sleeping so why would you pay for something you didn't do? Depending on how substantial the amount, there was probably more than one female involved.

Evidence: Your husband decides to leave you.

Excuse: "I just need some space," or "I just need to sort myself out."

Truth: This has got nothing to do with sorting himself out – it is an easy way to have a guilt-free affair. Once the affair is over he may decide he's sorted himself out and will want to come home.

Evidence: You find an empty packet of Viagra but haven't had sex for months.

Excuse: "I've been having some problems in that department lately."

Truth: Unless you have been living in separate universes surely you would know if there had been any problems in that department, and considering sex is a joint activity then you should have been part of the decision-making process.

Evidence: You find an eftpos receipt from a liquor store in another suburb not too far from home, corresponding to a day when he was supposed to be on a business trip out of town.

Excuse: "The date and time on the receipt is incorrect. It happen s all the time!"

Truth: He didn't go on that business trip out of town. He spent the night with his mistress.

Evidence: You find out that your husband has been on an internet dating site.

Excuse: "It was just a laugh between me and my mates at work to see what would happen and who would contact us."

Truth: Your husband is internet dating.

CHAPTER 4

Women Are Their Own Worst Enemies

Ask yourself this question: If you knew the guy you were about to marry was a lying, cheating, betraying, immature, deceiving, self-centered, insensitive jerk would you still marry him? I can hear you saying "Are you kidding? No way." So tell me, why is this kind of behavior all right now?

Women are their own worst enemies, and men know it and use that weakness to their advantage. And why not? You can't blame them because women allow it to happen.

Women are caring, nurturing creatures who are forever running around putting Band-Aids on dysfunctional relationships in the hope that they will heal the wounds, and that if they stay in a relationship long enough their partner will change into a monogamous husband. For God's sake, get your head out of the sand. Women need to toughen up and stand up for the right to be treated with respect.

It sounds so easy, and if you were to ask women if they respect themselves, of course they would say yes, but in reality that isn't always the case. I see the proof of that lack of respect daily. As a woman who does respect herself, it is the one aspect of my job that causes me the most frustration and sadness. I'm not going to say I haven't been where you are because I have, but the fundamental difference is that in the end I did something about it, whereas 95 per cent of my clients don't. I didn't sit back and excuse my husband's behavior because his father died when he was young and his childhood was less than idyllic. I didn't blame the other women for constantly enticing my husband away from me.

I did, however, sit back and think, "This has got nothing to do with me. I'm not the one with the problem. I've done nothing wrong." But initially I did something monumentally wrong all right – I believed him, I forgave him and I listened to all the excuses, and I thought, "You poor darling. How can I fix this?" So when I say I've been there you'd better believe I have, and when I say I know how to overcome this you had better believe that I do.

I'm going to keep on repeating this over and over again until you get it: love is a behavior, not just a feeling. When a man lies to you he is consciously disrespecting you. When he tells you he loves you his words are not enough. When a man lies to you his actions toward you and your relationship are lacking love. You can't gloss over it and make excuses-this is a fact. I find that when women excuse their husbands' lies, whatever those lies are about, in the end they are deluding themselves. There is nothing wrong with being compassionate and supportive, but it's destructive to support excuses when you know in your heart that's what you're doing.

So when I hear women tell me that apart from the fact that she can't trust her husband life is pretty good – because underneath it all he's a good husband, a great father and they have a good lifestyle, that he doesn't mean to be inconsiderate, that he's under pressure at work and is tired and stressed – I want to scream down the telephone, "Pull your head out of the sand; your justifications for his lack of respect just don't wash with me."

In fact, those women who telephone me because they have a problem have, by justifying their husbands' actions, talked themselves out of the reason for telephoning in the first place.

When you can justify his behavior so eloquently does it really matter that you hear a message from a woman on his cell phone saying that she's missing him, or you read a sexually graphic text message, or you can't contact him when he's away on business or you don't know where he's staying because he doesn't either? Of course it matters. You do yourself no favors by making excuses, because when someone has nothing to hide they hide nothing. Think about it. Do you forget where you go? Do you forget what you do? Of course you don't and nor does he, but for as long as you allow him to feed you this line of crap he'll keep on doing just that.

Now I can hear all the reasons why you can't do anything about this and why you have to accept this behavior. You have kids with this man, you've spent 25 years with this man, you can't imagine life on your own, and you can't imagine how you would survive financially. These reasons are all based on fear. Don't think for a minute I'm saying you have to leave, but make a stand and take back the power. Men know they have it over women, especially men who are deceiving their wives, because they know how vulnerable you are at this time. Don't tell me your husband's not like that. If he's lied to you he's like it all right.

We all have choices. When women make excuses and say they don't, what they are really saying is that they choose to stay in a contaminated relationship because they ultimately think it's easier all round. You have to recognize that if you do that you're not a victim – you are volunteering to put your health, sanity and inner peace in jeopardy, and I know this isn't what any woman wants to do; you don't need a psychologist to tell you that. We all want to have a monogamous relationship, but unless you make a stand you send a message out loud and clear that your feelings don't matter a jot. Most philandering men don't respect their wives' wishes, and if he sees that you don't treat yourself with respect either, he isn't about to change. Deceitful, lying, unfaithful men rarely become loving, trustworthy and faithful husbands, yet women stay in the hope that they will.

The answer is very, very simple: if you choose to stay in the knowledge that your husband has lied to you in the past and is lying to you now, and has only stopped the affair because he's been caught, has only gone to counseling because you asked him to, then you will experience stress and unhappiness as long as you're with this man. So don't complain, don't nag, and don't whine. Accept the choice you have made.

Women often talk about how they've supported their husbands emotionally and in many instances financially to help them get where they are today. I agree that the whole idea of marriage is to share a partnership, to respect and honor and most of all to be committed to each other. However, marriage shouldn't be about martyrdom and it shouldn't be to the detriment of either party's self-esteem or self-worth. As an example, one of my clients still makes her husband's lunch every day even though she's lived in a sexless marriage for 15 years (not of her choosing) and knows without doubt of two affairs he's had during their 32 years together. Yet she believes she's a strong and empowered woman who has been terribly wronged, and without doubt she has. But she is by no means an innocent player. Her role has been to make it easier for her husband to have the best of all worlds – his only problem has been listening to a bit of bitching and whining, which men are good at avoiding because they can turn a deaf ear when it suits them.

So what is it about women and martyrdom that seems to go hand in hand? A martyr is someone who suffers or dies for a cause or belief. Martyrs of years gone by were seen as strong people who gave hope and strength to others in their struggle for the right to practice their religious beliefs or speak their mind for a particular cause. Women who are the victims of infidelity and practice a form of martyrdom see themselves as strong women who are suffering for their cause, which is the family unit or their marriage. However, the problem is that this modern form of martyrdom isn't seen as strength by the husband but as a weakness — and a weakness to be exploited.

So then the women try to salvage the fast-sinking marriage by going over the same old ground time after time after time, regurgitating every detail. Yes, it's hard, and yes it hurts like hell, but reliving it over and over will not make it any better or any easier. In fact, it is more likely to provide him with justification for his infidelity because he can say, "God, is it any wonder I never come home when I have to listen to this broken record every day?"

Another classic guilt trip women try to use (but to no avail) is, "You just imagine what it would be like if the shoe was on the other foot. I bet you wouldn't hang around." This is a pretty stupid thing to say to a philanderer because he really couldn't care less which table his feet are under as long as some woman is looking after him. Once again a statement like this is seen as a weakness, because you can bet that if he was in the same situation he sure as hell wouldn't stay around.

Then there are the meaningless threats. You may ask why these threats are meaningless, and the answer is very simple — it's because they are never carried out.

"Don't worry, because from now on I'm going to watch him like a hawk." That's what a client said to me after we found her husband frequenting massage parlors after she had repeatedly told him this was unacceptable. The final straw was when she found a receipt in her son's trouser pocket for both his father and himself. My client had been married for 19 years and for most of those years her husband hadn't wanted to have an intimate relationship with her, but she hung in there, living in the hope that one day he would. When she confronted her husband with the receipt the only explanation he could come up with was, "We all do things we shouldn't; no one's perfect." So her life sentence is watching his every move. I'm sure you must be thinking why would you bother? Why would you waste valuable time on someone who is only going to do it again? Why, indeed? But nine out of ten women do.

So stop being a martyr and remember you can only change yourself-no one else. Forget about him for the time being and focus on yourself for a change. You make the choices in your life; don't live it for someone else, because you only get one crack at it (that we know of. Otherwise you'll end up living your life like the women in country and western songs – standing by your man.

Another example of how women can be their own worst enemies is when they find themselves living in sexless marriages, not because they have decided sex is not for them but because their husbands have made that decision for them. The reason that's usually given is that they (the husbands) are just not interested any more. Not only is this a hugely selfish attitude, but it's surprising they're allowed to get away with it. The majority of these marriages are of 20 to 30 years' duration and in some cases the husband and wife still sleep in the same bed, although many men in these circumstances decide to leave the matrimonial bed in favor of a single bed in the spare room.

Jan is one of my long-standing clients (she's been a client

as long as I have been in business). Jan has been long-suffering and for a decade has lived in a sexless marriage. And before you start telling me that sex isn't everything in a relationship let me remind you of what I said at the outset: if you have a good sexual relationship sex is about 15 per cent on the scale of importance. However, if you don't have a good sexual relationship, or your relationship (as in the case of Jan) is devoid of sex, then that's about 95 per cent on the scale of importance. The sad truth for Jan was that her husband was having regular sex with prostitutes and had been for 13 years. The reason that he had removed himself emotionally, physically and sexually from Jan was that for those 13 years she had lived out a fantasy. So he lost the ability to have a satisfying and fulfilling relationship with his wife.

This book is not about your husband, although it may sound as if it is – it is about you. Please don't get defensive because the truth is hard to hear. The fact is that if you want to change your relationship you have to start with yourself first, from top to toe and from inside out. You have to take the power back and become the sort of person who commands respect, who will not settle for less than being treated with dignity and abiding love by the person you've chosen as your partner.

Women will always come up with an excuse or reason for accepting inappropriate behavior in their marriage. Take, for instance, Kelly, whose husband George frequented massage parlors, spending hundreds of dollars a week. She took the view that frequenting prostitutes wasn't as bad as if he were having an affair. I've always had trouble coming to grips with this way of thinking, because sex is sex when all is said and done. It's not as

though the prostitute would do less than the wife. In fact, she is sure to do more. What Kelly is really saying is that because there's no emotional connection then it's not as dangerous or threatening to her marriage. Again Kelly, like so many women, is assuming George is thinking how she would think if she were in an extramarital relationship, i.e., it would have to be emotionally as well as physically driven. However, for most men affairs aren't driven by an emotional connection but a physical one – he is only interested in the person he is having the affair with for sex, which is no different from when he visits a prostitute. So what is the difference between him having an affair with the office junior and buying her presents and dinners, and paying money to a prostitute? I would suggest none, because what he wants from both is exactly the same – sex.

There may be times as you're reading this book when you might think, "This woman is a shrew." But if I am to be absolutely truthful with you and myself, there's no easy way for me to give you the cold hard facts as I see them. Most of the people who become my clients are in some form of therapy. Whether they are seeing a marriage counselor or a psychologist makes no difference; the fact is they are in serious emotional trouble and, from where I sit, making very little progress – if any at all. When someone is smack in the middle of something as destructive as being continually lied to by the one person they expect to be able to trust, the effects are physically and emotion-

ally devastating. It's easy to pussyfoot around this issue by taking months and in many cases even years to come to some sort of understanding and acknowledgement, but the longer you take to get a handle on it the more damage you're doing to yourself and those around you. There are so many factors to consider, including the risk to your health, because you don't know the sexual history of your husband's new sex partner. So many times children are born out of casual relationships. This can bring about a whole different set of problems, including the possibility that the children of your marital relationship could end up marrying a child of the illicit relationship.

The effect an affair has on the children of a marriage cannot be discounted, and don't think for a minute that they will be oblivious to what's going on. Often it's the children who pay the highest price, especially in marriages of long duration, because over the years they will have noticed the changes in how their parents interact with each other. They will have noticed the tension and understood the innuendo. They will have overheard many a supposedly private conversation.

Remember, certain behaviors are learnt, and when children grow up in this sort of environment a boy learns that you can have your cake and eat it too. He learns that although he may suffer some minor irritations along the way, all his meals will be cooked, his laundry will be done and everyone else will think he's an OK kind of guy. On the other hand, the message a girl gets is that this is the way men behave, and if you want all the nice trappings it's the price you have to pay. Is this what you want your children to learn?

One of the worst things I think people tend to do in situations of infidelity is not to talk about it with anyone. I'm not suggesting you have to go into all the gory details, but in saying nothing you are effectively condoning the behavior. I have a client who has had so much proof of infidelity that it's staggering and yet she always finds an excuse to stay. Every time she finds another indiscretion she pushes the line in the sand further and further away. Her continual confrontations regarding receipts and notes found in his wallet and diary show him what not to do in the future and compound her lonely living hell, because her words don't correspond with actions. I've noticed her turn into a bitter and resentful woman, and if I have seen it surely her friends and family have seen it too, yet I know she hasn't told a living soul apart from me. So her husband remains on a pedestal in the eyes of all who know him and he's never had to take responsibility for his actions.

You can see why men continue to betray; the price they have to pay is never high enough.

Women need to strike while the iron is hot because there comes a time (and that time has arrived for this client) when spilling the beans would reflect on her credibility. No one would understand why, with all the information she's had over such a long period, she's never told anyone or taken any action before now.

Another sad example that shows how misguided and weak women can be is Tina, who is more than financially secure – if she left her husband she would be able to afford more than three freehold homes and have money to spare, yet she chooses to stay in an emotional prison.

I've thought about Tina many times and have come to an under standing of her situation. Like the woman in the previous example, Tina has had more than enough proof of her husband Karl's indiscretions over a long period of time. For a number of years she's had access to his email account and she's found details of an affair, including messages to and from his lover regarding flight schedules and holidays they were planning when he was supposed to be away on business. We even caught him with his lover in a country hideaway close to home when he had vowed and declared to his wife he just needed time alone to sort himself out once and for all. This after Tina had issued the grand ultimatum that if he lied one more time it was all over. But on his return he said he wanted to make a go of it and was committed to his marriage. He also initiated sex with her – in a variation on an old theory that "Men use love to get sex and women use sex to get love." What Karl was doing was not too different in that the sex he initiated with Tina was sending her the signal that he wanted her, therefore tying her into him yet again.

All the time I have been writing this book my phone has never stopped ringing with people experiencing all forms of betrayal. I had a delightful woman ring and ask me what I thought was enough evidence before she took some action. I explained to her that she would have to come to that conclusion herself, but I asked her to give me some examples of what had been happening.

All through our married life my husband Sam has been

hooked on the idea of threesomes and group sex. It had never appealed to me but after years of pressure I finally gave in — it was the worst thing I could ever have done because he continually asks for it to happen again, not only with another woman but now with another man, and I'm sure this is due to behavioral patterns that show he may be bisexual. On a number of occasions I have found him in sex chat rooms arranging to meet both men and women, and he has swags of porn magazines in his car.

I let her continue, and all the time I was thinking, "What more does she think she needs?" This isn't what marriage is all about unless both parties have agreed to it without pressure of any kind. It wasn't what this woman wanted or had agreed to without pressure, and therefore showed no respect for her or their relationship. I asked her if this was what she had expected her marriage to be like when she got married, to which she answered, "No, but all men want a threesome don't they?" I replied, "Not all men, but granted a lot do. However, most married men would only think about it."

She was somewhat taken aback by my answer because for 25 years she had been programmed into thinking she was the one with the problem. This was because whenever she told her husband she felt uncomfortable in this type of situation he made her feel guilty by suggesting that by not wanting to participate she was spoiling his enjoyment. Surely his behavior and lack of respect was enough evidence to begin with?

Long before you ever encounter betrayal, you need to have some absolutely watertight rules in place about what you will and will not accept. Not what society tells you to accept, but what you truly believe you can live with. To believe in your self-worth takes a strong person. Most of my clients think it's easier to stay in a contaminated marriage than to go, but I know that with any abuse in the long run it is easier to leave. Surely it's better to be free to pursue one's own dreams than to stay in a marriage with a man that is a marriage in name only?

When a woman chooses to stay with a man she knows is a repeat philanderer and he does eventually leave, as many do after years of marriage, she feels slighted for having put up with his behavior for the best part of her life. Women find all sorts of reasons for staying in a marriage. When a woman finds that all the love and devotion she has shown her husband hasn't changed him, and that waiting for him to change is a naive notion, she comforts herself by choosing reasons for staying such as:

- She loves her husband.
- She loves her children and family.
- She enjoys the lifestyle they have.
- She holds the opinion that all men cheat.
- She could never trust another man.
- Why would she give her husband to another woman?
- Who would want her now?
- Women of a certain social standing need a husband.
- She is financially bound to the relationship.

Key points

- Believe in yourself.
- Know your self-worth.
- Have clear boundaries in place.

- Do not accept being bullied or persuaded into doing something you feel is wrong.
- Put yourself first.
- Build a loving relationship with yourself.
- Above all else respect yourself.

Virtue—a blessing or a curse?

I have included this subject here because while virtue is the very thing that throughout the centuries men have wanted in their wives, many men use virtue against women. In years gone by it was seen as a sign of virtue for a woman to enter marriage without any sexual experience, and many of my clients have had cause to question this many years down the track.

This interesting fact has come to light due to the increasing numbers of women who, having been married to the same man for 25-plus years, are now the victims of infidelity. They've told me how the very fact that they were inexperienced sexually when they married has in many instances worked against them. It is a fact of life, and one I can back up through my clients, that the men these women married had had far more sexual partners and experience than the virtuous woman they married. And so, with the level of sexual experience stacked so heavily against these women, it has been easy for their husbands to manipulate the situation to suit themselves, knowing their wives have nothing to compare them with. This has led to these sexually naive women being sexually conditioned by their husband s. As hard as it is to believe in this day and age, 50 per cent of my female clients have been sexually conditioned by sexually dysfunctional men. Dysfunctional may be a strong word to use, but these men are living out sexual fantasies and conditioning their wives into thinking this is normal. There would be no problem if their wives were comfortable with participating. However, this is not the case.

A large number of the women I deal with think it's normal for their husbands to place adverts in the paper looking for strangers to take part in threesomes. They think it's normal that their husbands want to attend sex clubs while on holiday, or say that the only sexual satisfaction they can get is through anal sex. The women do these things not because they want to but because they feel this is the way to keep their husbands. I know it sounds incredible considering that these women are usually in their forties and are the wives of professional men , but as I have said many times it's all about communication and people just don't feel comfortable discussing sex. There is no doubt that these women are at the opposite end of the spectrum from today's "out there" single female who's had many sexual partners and has analyzed every part of her various lovers' anatomies and lovemaking techniques with her girlfriends.

Many of the women who become my clients have a warped view of sex. They tell me they think all men are unfaithful, all men are into porn, all men demand group sex and all men are sexually deviant, to which I reply that not all men are but if your man is and you are comfortable with it, then that's fine. But if your man is this way and doesn't care whether you are comfortable or not, then I cannot stress enough how important it is not to accept such behavior. You must not roll over and allow your man to dominate, but stand up and accept only what you feel comfortable with.

Guilt trip

Why is it that women who have been constantly lied to, deceived and betrayed feel guilty when they finally decide to take steps to find out the truth about their marriage? I've had women say to me: "This is wrong, I shouldn't be doing this to him," or, "I feel so bad. He would kill me if he found out," and "I can't believe I'm doing this. I feel so guilty."

Knowledge is power and you have every right to know what's been happening in your marriage. In fact, it is extremely irresponsible not to make an effort to know, because very often it's not just your emotional well-being at risk, it can be your financial well-being and even your physical safety. What about sexually transmitted diseases, or STDs – is your husband safe? One of my clients picked up an STD this way, so for goodness sake stop feeling guilty because of his actions and start taking responsibility for yourself.

Then I have women telling me how much better they feel just by sharing the problem with someone, taking action and knowing they are no longer accepting his lies. The reason women bury their heads in the sand is fear, because if they knew what was going on they would feel obliged to do something about it. The more you know, the more able you are to protect yourself. I don't mean you have to end your marriage there and then, but having that knowledge allows you to make choices and to decide what you want to do for your future happiness. Having that knowledge can also help put your mind at rest. It can reassure you that you aren't going crazy. Many women feel this way after confronting their husband s, because these men usually try to transfer the blame and make it their wives' fault. A man may suggest it's all in your mind, and say he can't handle forever being accused of something he hasn't done. This behavior is very typical of someone who has been caught out, but by having information and knowledge you don't have to take his guilt on board. Even if he never admits to any wrongdoing (and many don't), at least you know in your heart the true facts – and that's power.

Some clients feel so guilty and ashamed about doing something that they have every right to do that they get a friend or family member to deal with me, another action which is driven by fear. If you choose to live in fear you cannot possibly grow, and you therefore give the perpetrator of the infidelity control.

Key points

- Cast out your guilt and fear and remember just who is the problem.
- Don't ever have unprotected sex with a philandering husband.
- Never ever feel guilty about standing up for your rights.
- Take the power back, because knowledge is power.
- If you need help from a professional don't use a relative or friend to telephone on your behalf. Only you know the intimate details of your relationship and it is often those details that are the key for me. Remember that second-hand information loses much in the transfer.

Leave it to the professionals

If you do suspect your partner of infidelity, whether you have caught him out in the past or it's just a gut feeling, don't invest all your time and energy in finding out by trying to do the job yourself because it will end up consuming you.

I have watched women drop dress sizes through burning up all that nervous energy. It may sound like a quick fix for a weight problem but believe me; losing weight through stress only leaves you drawn and haggard. I also find that when someone tries to do their own detective work they become obsessed and often focus on the wrong issues, missing vital clues. Someone like me, a professional investigator, brings objectivity to a case, which understandably you cannot have when you are so emotionally affected. Clients become so preoccupied by worrying about their husband's every move that they have no time for themselves anymore and become worn out.

The next and probably most destructive element of trying to play detective is that clients end up prolonging the inevitable simply by spilling the beans every time they get a piece of key evidence. Instead of keeping quiet until they have a plan of action they challenge and confront their partner, which in turn alerts their deceitful spouse that he is being monitored so he knows what not to do in the future. If you do confront your partner before you have an action plan then you have achieved nothing except to send a message loud and clear that says, "Hey, you go right ahead and have sex with whoever you like and I'll still be here." So don't show your hand until you have evidence (catching them out lying is enough) and a plan in mind for your future.

I've lost count of the number of clients I've interviewed and asked, "Are you sure you've told me everything?" – only to be told, after working on their case and discussing our findings, "I knew that already." The importance of releasing all information, no matter how personal or embarrassing you may find it, allows us to achieve optimum results.

Another pet frustration is the client who wants to play junior detective and decides to help by turning up while we're on surveillance. The last thing we want anywhere near the subject is the client, and an emotionally charged one at that.

Key points

- Don't hold back on information because it's embarrassing to you. We've heard it all before and are non-judgmental.
- Don't try and "out-detective" us. The police don't allow civilians on undercover jobs and neither do we.
- Don't keep spilling the beans; use your smarts. Play it close to your chest until you have the evidence required.

Intimidation tactics

You finally have a confession after endless denials. The evidence has been too overwhelming for him to keep dodging and he has nowhere else to hide, so his only option has been to fess up and admit defeat-he's been having an affair with a married work colleague. Your first response is to say: "Right, you get rid of her or I'm telling her husband he's married to a slut." He reacts by saying, "Go right ahead, and let it be on your conscience that you've destroyed a marriage. What do you hope to achieve? Why ruin two people's lives? It's not her fault; I'm to blame. Leave her out of this." Reactions such as this are born out of:

- wanting to protect his lover;
- fear;
- weakness and cowardice;
- utter disrespect.

You can see that he wants to protect his lover because he is looking after her feelings in preference to yours, which is really no surprise because he didn't care about your feelings to begin with – otherwise this affair would never have occurred. He's also afraid of her husband finding out and any repercussions either for himself or for his lover.

Weakness and cowardice are obvious because most men will do anything to avoid looking bad, especially in front of friends and colleagues, and they will often use intimidation tactics to try to get their accuser to back down. The example above shows the husband is planting the blame firmly at his wife's feet, suggesting that if she phones his lover's husband and reveals the affair it will be her fault for breaking up the marriage. He is attempting to divert attention from his wrongdoing onto his wife. So if you find yourself facing any of these reactions look him straight in the eye and say: "Listen, buddy, you can come up with every fancy maneuvers under the sun; you can transfer guilt, shift the blame, minimize and justify, whatever turns you on, but I'm not buying any of it because the fact is you did this; you got yourself into this mess. You deliberately put our marriage in jeopardy. You thought this affair through and executed it – so grow up, be a man and take responsibility for your actions."

He won't expect you to be so direct. You may even throw him off balance, but you need to be tough and resolute to deal with his bullshit, because that's all this is. And when you get tough he will know it's pointless trying to elicit your sympathy, which is probably his next avenue of attack.

The sympathy card

I can still hear Anne's voice when she said to me, "What have I done? You don't think I've driven him to suicide, do you?"

All Anne had been guilty of was confronting her philandering husband about his latest dalliance, but David decided to do what he'd always done in situations like this and play "Mr Pathetic". He turned on the tears and begged Anne to forgive him, because this behavior had kept him out of trouble in the past. By playing on her sympathy he was hoping Anne would forgive him and fall straight back into his arms as she'd always done before. The reason this had worked so well for David was that he wasn't normally an emotional man, so to see him in such a state was upsetting for Anne. Every time he did this she believed he was truly sorry for his deeds. But we all have a breaking point and Anne had finally reached hers.

This was the fourth time David had been unfaithful (that Anne knew it, but this time she was more upset than on any of the previous occasions because for the first time she'd actually stood up to him and he could see that all his ranting and raving was having little effect. He had stormed out of the house, leaving her with the parting shot, "I've had it. I can't take any more of this. That's it, it's over."

Anne was obviously serious when she asked me if I thought David would take his own life. My reply was, "He's playing with you – he thinks he knows you so well that he'll know what you're thinking and how you'll react – but to answer your question: no, I don't think he'll kill himself – it takes guts to commit suicide and your husband is gutless."

If you hear responses such as these he's using the sympathy card:

- "OK, so I lied, but that doesn't mean I don't love you."
- "You have no idea how bad I feel."
- "How can you do this to us?"
- "I can't take this anymore."

Don't fall for this manipulation, because the minute he gets you back on side you'll be straight back to square one. Please don't lose sight of the fact that without honesty and respect in a relationship, these being the two essential ingredient s, there can be no moving forward.

Covering his tracks by taking advantage of female sensibilities

Often, men who are betraying will sow a seed when they are either running two relationships or you're getting too close to uncovering their secret, because there's always the possibility they will be exposed.

What better way to "cover their ass" than by pre-empting the situation and getting in first with a heart-wrenching story about some terrible physical or emotional illness that's affecting them, the other woman, her family or his family? If there is anything that will make a woman back off it's a play on her female sensibilities. This is because it's not in the nature of women (the nurturers and caregivers) to cause undue stress for anyone who is suffering.

This particular type of manipulation is used time and again. Why? Because it works. So if you hear some tragic story from a man you've just met, or your husband or partner who continues to take his attention away from you, don't accept all that is said as gospel. Get some facts. You will more than likely find that if he says he's having health issues himself these may well be born out of the fear that you're getting too close. This type of man only wants part of a relationship and not the whole. On the other hand, if the supposed health issues relate to a female friend of his, he is simply playing on your sympathies. With a little research you'll no doubt find she hasn't been diagnosed with cancer, she doesn't have severe psychological problems, she hasn't tried to kill herself lately and her father isn't in hospital with severe heart problems. In fact, the only person in this story with severe problems is the person telling it to you!

Key points

- Don't allow him to shift or divert the blame.
- Be direct and bring the subject back to the fact that he's responsible for his actions, and that for every action there is a reaction.
- If he rants and raves or storms out keep a cool head and refer him back to the previous point.

- If he tries for sympathy have your boundaries firmly set and remind him that it's you who has been hurt and no matter how bad he feels it is nothing in comparison to the pain you have been dealt.

CHAPTER 5

Human Nature Is A Curious Thing

The old saying "Beauty is in the eye of the beholder" couldn't be more true. It doesn't seem to make any difference if they are male or female; one of the first things I hear when a client calls is how attractive their partner is. At the beginning of my career I can remember a male client describing his wife as a stunningly beautiful woman, and he seemed to half-expect her to have admirers everywhere she went. Although he was incredibly hurt by her infidelity he made it sound as if it was something that had just been waiting to happen. I immediately had an image of Elle Macpherson in my mind. I asked for a recent photograph, part of the usual information I collect from a client, which he duly sent to me. I was completely taken aback when I saw the photo of his wife. She was a pleasant-enough-looking woman, a little on the plump side, with short salt-and-pepper hair. When I phoned my client to say I'd received the information he said, "Well, you can see what I mean, she's beautiful, isn't she?" To which I replied politely, "Yes, she's lovely."

If you think about this it makes perfect sense because one of the vital factors when choosing a mate is physical attraction. What's interesting is that these people believe that everyone else sees their partner in the same light as they do. Nine out of ten of my clients will make reference to their partner's good looks. For example, a woman will say, "My husband is a very good-looking man," or "My husband is a very charismatic man." Men, on the other hand, will say, "My wife is a very beautiful woman," or "My wife is a gorgeous-looking girl."

I will never forget one client who sent me a photo of her philandering, supposedly charismatic and handsome husband; he was standing with a group of six other guys at a barbecue. They were all big men with rather large stomachs – I couldn't tell one charismatic man from another. However, there was a particularly unattractive man in the centre, and when I turned the photo over my client had written on the back: "Bob's the one in the middle". This only confirms that beauty is firmly in the eye of the beholder.

Interestingly enough, women take this one step further when con fronted with their husband's infidelity. At this stage these men are not only incredibly handsome but extremely clever in their wives' eyes, because how else could they have got away with it?

But in truth, even if he were as good-looking as David Beckham (whom I consider handsome) he could have all the women in the world throwing their bodies at him but that wouldn't mean he had to do anything about it. Only your man is responsible for his actions. No one can make him have sex with her against his will, although it's easier to cope if you believe your poor husband has been seduced into having an affair. And as for him being so clever, what can I say? If you are on to him, how clever can he really be? This is another way of coping with the fact that you've chosen to believe someone who has lied to you. Women try to obtain comfort by shifting the blame for their husband's infidelity. As furious as they are when they know that their husband has deliberately chosen to deceive them, they accuse the other woman of enticing their husband away. Intellectually you know that unless the recipient is willing to be enticed then it can't happen, and notwithstanding your marriage contract with your husband the other woman is under no obligation to you. Particularly if the woman is single, she can do who and what she chooses. Of course, morally she shouldn't be looking for a married man, but she isn't your problem. Your husband was the one who pledged to forsake all others and show you respect – so don't lose sight of the fact that he's made a conscious decision to betray you. A truly clever man knows better than to go down this path, so don't give him credit where it isn't due.

I had a client some years ago whose husband started taking Viagra to enhance their sex life. He had it by the truckload – in the bathroom, in the garage, in the boot of his car – and when he went overseas on business he would put the distinctive blue pills into an empty vitamin bottle. Unbeknown to him his wife was monitoring every disappearing tablet because she knew not one of those pills was used for her. She said to me, "How can I prove he's cheating on me? He's so clever, because each time he uses one he replaces it with another." What we have here is not so much the act of a clever man, but the actions of a stupid woman.

Key points

- Just because you find your partner attractive don't assume the rest of the world does.
- If your intuition makes you feel that your partner is betraying you then he's not clever – your unconscious mind has already picked up on the signs.
- Stop putting yourself down and making excuses for your partner's behavior. It's not your fault. He is shifting the blame, so let him know that you will not take responsibility for his actions. However, if you do continue to accept this behavior then you have to accept your part in it.

One minute he's there and then he's gone

I'm sure you will be just as surprised as I was to learn how many men walk out on their wives and families, seemingly with no warning. The first time I heard of this was when a client explained to me that her husband was on medication for depression and had been depressed on and off throughout the 26 years they had been married. But at this time he had actually seemed more settled than he had been in the past. He had been mowing the lawns when he ran out of fuel, so he called out to his wife to let her know he was just going to the local garage to get some more. It was about 20 minutes later that she looked out the window and saw the lawnmower sitting where he'd left it, but no sign of her husband. Twenty-four hours later she reported him missing to the police. He had gone with only the clothes he was wearing and, as far as she knew, very little money. Eight months later there had been no contact, nor had any money been taken from their joint account. Some ten months after his disappearance she finally received a letter from him apologizing for all the pain he'd caused and explaining that he now lived in another town and wouldn't be returning home.

He's now in a new relationship and hasn't formally told his children or had any contact with them. His wife was left to wind down their business and try to put what was left of her life in some semblance of order. We've kept in touch over the years and it's been a long hard haul for her but she's now doing well. The matrimonial property has been settled in her favor, as he wanted nothing. The only explanation she had from him was that he was dissatisfied with his life.

From that time until now cases of this kind have kept coming, but it's interesting to note we've never had a woman do this to her family.

Another client told me her husband went out one Saturday afternoon to buy the weekly lottery ticket and never returned. This wasn't the first time he'd done this in their 28-year marriage, so when he hadn't returned after an hour she had a sinking feeling that history was about to repeat itself. Although this man had a very responsible job he was prone to mood swings, had gone off with other women in the past and had stayed away for months at a time, but he would always return eventually, saying how much he'd missed her. For my client this time was the last straw. She explained to me that the most frustrating part of trying to cope with it was that he never gave any explanation as to why he did this. As it's not a common situation to find yourself in, those around you won't really be able to offer much help, which leaves you extremely vulnerable and isolated. This man could see the devastation he caused but it was never enough to stop him.

Men who leave with somewhere and someone to go to

I'll never forget Denise's call. She said:

I've been married to an absolute bastard for 30 years. He's just walked out, telling me he doesn't feel we have anything in common any more. I wonder when he came to that conclusion. He's been a bloody great bully all our married life. He'll bonk any female who crosses his path and I have put up with hell for years, and now he just decides he's going to go and start a new life. What about me? What am I expected to do? He swears black and blue there's no one else; he just can't stand being around me any longer. I bet you've never heard of this before.

Before I could answer Denise was off again:

He'll not get away with this. I haven't spent the last 30 years doing his dirty laundry just to sit back and let that bastard dictate to me. I have no idea where he's gone to, he wouldn't tell me, but I need you to find out. He's got to come back here this weekend to pick up the rest of his clothes so I thought you could follow him from here and see where he goes.

To respond to Denise's statement ("I bet you've never heard of this before"), I think it's fair to say I've heard everything before. It's impossible to do my job and not hear stories like this over and over again. That's where my knowledge has come from.

We did follow Denise's husband that weekend and he led us to a modest apartment in a trendy and expensive part of the city. A few minutes later a woman arrived driving his other vehicle and punched in the security code to the underground parking area. One of my investigators had found a superb vantage point on an adjacent street with uninterrupted views of the apartment's balcony and lounge area, where it was very easy to observe Denise's husband and his lover. It turned out that they were very serious about their relationship and had been for quite some time, so much so that they'd bought property overseas some months earlier and moved there to set up home only a few days after we watched them.

Jen was another long-suffering wife and had been married

to John, an international airline pilot, for 32 years. His lifestyle gave him enormous opportunity to play the field and he took full advantage of it. Like most men who deceive, John wasn't particularly good at it, and Jen was on to it right from the start. She knew of five affairs, all of long duration, that John had conducted, and countless one-night stands, but like Denise she'd done nothing about it other than relentlessly berating him, using threats that never materialized. John got to the point where he just turned off, knowing she would never kick him out as she threatened to do. As long as he could cope with the torrent of abuse hurled at him, life wasn't too bad. The end came when John started having an affair with a senior member of his cabin crew and finally told Jen he'd had enough of her constant moaning and was moving out. Truth was, John had fallen in love. However, that didn't last and he moved out again just a week later. John now lives alone and sees both women periodically.

The statistics say that only five per cent of such relationships stand the test of time. Women like Denise and Jen who live with men who are repeat offenders in the infidelity stakes run the risk of their partner leaving. Choosing to stay in a relationship riddled with infidelity must have a pay-off, and for these women the pay-off was lifestyle. But men who have essentially been dating all their married life and are at an age where they are prepared to take a gamble only leave if they have somewhere and someone to go to. It is important that women put more emphasis not on how much love they give their husbands but on how much love they receive in return. Women believe that if they hang on to him at all costs and love him, he'll do the same, but this behavior doesn't guarantee faithfulness or even the reciprocation of love.

Jerry Hall springs to mind as a woman who's travelled down this path, loving and constantly forgiving Mick Jagger through all his betrayals. Not his children or even their history together was enough to deter Mick from his philandering ways. Mick and Jerry are no longer together but Mick found somewhere soft to fall.

Not all women are as fortunate. Jerry Hall is beautiful, famous, rich and successful in her own right and therefore has a greater range of opportunities than many of my clients, who often don't see themselves as strong, attractive and vital women. Women cling to the commonly held belief that if they can sit it out long enough one day he will grow out of his philandering ways. I'm afraid to say, ladies, that you are deluding yourselves and in doing so you are essentially giving away your life to a man who will never change no matter how much time you give him. It's true that leopards don't change their spots, just as frogs don't turn into princes. It's a sad fact that once a philanderer always a philanderer, so don't waste precious time waiting for him to change; it won't happen because he doesn't want it to. This sort of behavior is a habit and these men have always been like this in varying degrees. Whether you choose to acknowledge it is up to you.

Think about it like this. Do you start every day with a coffee? If you do, that's a habit. If someone said you weren't allowed that coffee you would realize how important it was to you. If you were then told you would never be able to have coffee again I'm sure you would think, "I could do that, but really what's the issue? It's only coffee." So, before long you would revert back to your morning coffee.

Men who betray don't put any more emphasis on their infidelities than you do on your morning coffee. Your partner doesn't see it as a big problem — it's you who does that — to him it's only sex, it doesn't mean anything. And he's still looking after you (financially) and he hasn't left you (yet). Just like you with your coffee, he may be able to stop for a while but eventually he'll revert to type.

The reason he can and often will leave is because he's disconnected from you. If he had any care and consideration for you at all he wouldn't have behaved like this to start with. So just as you could change from coffee to tea, if he had wanted he could have concentrated on his life with you rather than pursuing other women.

The only way to change a habit is if you really want to and are 100 per cent committed. You must acknowledge you are changing for yourself and the way it will better you, and not someone else — otherwise it won't work. It's like an alcoholic going to AA because his wife has asked him to stop drinking — it's not going to work because it's his wife who wants him to stop, not he himself.

So if you are living with a serial betrayer don't spend the rest of your life trying to change or even trust him — concentrate on trusting yourself to make the right decisions for you in the future.

Girl power

I have been saying for years that women are not so different from men when it comes to their desire for sex. Men believe they have the monopoly in that area, which is partly out of arrogance and partly the result of social conditioning. They really believe their partner would never cheat on them. However, women are not as demure and naive as men think, because when it comes to infidelity women leave men for dead in terms of the planning and execution of an affair.

Just as many women betray their husbands as men betray their wives. The only difference from my point of view is that I work mainly for women. That tells you one thing: women get away with it far more than men do, and there are many reasons for this. Firstly, women today have far more independence than they ever had in the past. One behavioral trait in betrayers is that they are opportunists, and with so many women out in the workforce they are now faced with opportunities not available to women 30 years ago. They don't just sit around waiting for their men to come home. In fact, quite often it's the other way round.

Women today are emotionally and socially stronger than ever before and know that if their marriage does break down they have the wherewithal to survive. Also contraception plays a major role, giving women sexual freedom. Women are also staying sexier for longer (hallelujah) than in the old days. In the past, if you weren't dead at 40 you certainly weren't seen as a sexual being, but now we're living longer and with hormone replacement therapy (HRT) there is no reason that anything has to change. I have had many clients in their sixties and seventies with very healthy sexual appetites.

The revenge affair

Women are very capable of having an affair as revenge when they've been deceived by their partners, more capable in fact than many men ever realize. And a woman will plan her affair more meticulously than any man; she will usually have a back-up plan and a girlfriend who will cover for her. While a woman may sometimes choose to ignore her intuition, men have suppressed their intuitive skills to the point where they rarely use them. Again, this is to a woman's advantage when covering her tracks. If you likened the sexes' intuition on infidelity to a runaway train hurtling down the tracks, a woman would sense the danger before hearing the train but a man would probably only know the train was there when it ran him over.

Sally was married to a man who lied like a flatfish. She had been suspicious of him for years but could never prove anything – well, anything that would satisfy her. However, she did have copies of his mobile phone bill – they were suspicious all right – there was a number he phoned consistently. In fact, he was ringing it every morning as he pulled out of his driveway. What disturbed Sally was that the number belonged to her best friend. But what really rang alarm bells was what happened one night when Sally and her husband were on their way out to dinner. They pulled up at a liquor store and Sally waited in the car while her husband went in to buy some wine.

Why she looked in the glove compartment she doesn't really know, but what she found there was the infidelity version of a smoking gun: packets of Viagra, lots of them. Sally saw there were some tablets missing, but she knew they hadn't come near her! From then on Sally monitored the tablets and employed my company to stake out her friend's house in the mornings when her husband left for work.

One of my investigators stationed himself outside Sally's friend's house. He quickly realized that the reason Sally's husband was ringing her best friend as he pulled out of his driveway each morning was to check whether the coast was clear at the other end. No sooner had Sally's friend's husband left for work than my investigator saw Sally's husband pull into her driveway. When she opened the door for him she was still dressed in her PJs, and Sally's husband fondled her breast as he walked in the door and disappeared inside.

Sally asked us to observe for a few more days to establish a pattern so that her husband wouldn't be able to lie his way out of this affair as he had several times in the past. Once she had the evidence she was obviously furious, and she said to me, "I'll show the bastard; he's not going to treat me like a fool and get away with it – he'll rue the day he walked through that door – I haven't finished with him yet."

It was a couple of months later when I got another call from Sally, and she sounded like a different woman – there was laughter in her voice as she told me she'd sorted her husband out. She'd presented him with the evidence and now he was walking around with his tail between his legs.

But she wasn't about to stop there – Sally wanted revenge. Like many of my clients she didn't want to leave her marriage; she felt the money and lifestyle were too good to let go. Sally put an ad in the personal column of the newspaper looking for a man to have discreet sex with, and to her amazement she received 200 replies from just one small advertisement. The men who wrote to her ranged in age from 19 to 80, and she narrowed them down to 30 potential lovers.

Then , every morning after waving her husband off to work , Sally would spend hours bathing , preening and dressing herself up to the nines before going out to interview her potential playmates at discreet cafes about town. She was having the time of her life. After a little bit of deliberation those 30 candidates became five, and those lucky five became her lovers. Laughing, she said to me, "My husband is so stupid. He thought he was so clever having his little fling right under my nose, but he's absolutely oblivious to what I'm getting up to while he's slogging it out at work every day!"

I actually think there is a time and place when a revenge affair can be beneficial. It may sound shocking to hear me suggesting that you should even consider such a thing, but this is about real life and there really is no right or wrong way to act or react in these situations. It's a matter of trial and error for each one of us. But when life goes haywire, as in dealing with infidelity and its aftermath, it's whatever helps you through that counts. This is where female virtue can be a hindrance rather than a help. "Two wrongs don't make a right, but they make a good excuse", as Thomas Szasz has said.

I've often asked my clients if they would ever consider having an affair after the discovery of infidelity, and the answer is usually an overwhelming "No! I could never do that!" Well, ladies, maybe you should — there's a lot of power to be gained out of sex: it works for some and it sure worked for me!

In the two years I stayed in my first hellish marriage, and for two years after it ended, I had an affair. I didn't regret it then, and nearly forty years later when I think about it, it still brings a smile to my face. One of my clients said that when she went to bed with her lover after her husband had betrayed her for the third time, she "felt the shackles breaking and a new freedom beginning". Just like me, she didn't stay in her marriage or with her lover; her affair was a catalyst in discovering that she deserved a better life.

 *The cruelest lies are often told in silence: Robert Louis Stevenson*

Let me give you another real-life example of female revenge at its most creative. I have a very wealthy, attractive client in her late sixties, who has hired me over the years for a very unusual task. One week in every year she employs my company to watch her husband rigorously: from the time he leaves home in the morning until the time he comes back at night, my operatives are on his tail. Why? Well, let me tell you. Some years ago this woman discovered her husband and her very best girlfriend were having an affair, but unlike most of my clients, she didn't confront them there and then – she didn't get mad, she did something quite different.

You see, like Sally, this woman had no intention of walking out on her husband – as she told me, she had too much to lose: they were a high-profile couple – the prospect of the public humiliation a divorce would bring was too much to contemplate – and there was the matter of the lifestyle she felt she'd lose if she left.

But what she could, and did, do was get even, just for herself. About a year after her secret discovery she went skiing on her own at Lake Tahoe USA, where she met a very nice young attorney. One thing led to another, and eventually the attorney started coming to New Zealand to ski in our winter. And for one week of every holiday he goes to my client's house every day after her husband leaves for work and spends the day with her in bed. My client hires our company to make sure her husband doesn't come home unexpectedly and catch them. The irony, of course, is that the husband's affair ended long ago, and his wife's little secret has continued for over seven years.

Whether you think it's right or wrong, deceiving her husband the way he deceived her is how one woman deals with infidelity, and that's what matters to her.

So you can see, some women seek revenge in a very underhand way. Another example of this is a client whose discovery of her husband's infidelity resulted in his moving into their holiday apartment with his lover, leaving the wife in the family home. While the husband and his lover were away overseas, the vengeful wife let herself into the apartment, scattered grass seed over the lovely shagpile carpet and proceeded to water it. On their return, the husband and lover were greeted with a beautifully lush knee-high lawn.

A further example of a vengeful wife was a woman who, following the untimely death of her husband, discovered at the funeral that he had a lover and love child. Several months after her husband's cremation and the return of his ashes, her children were concerned that their father's ashes had not been scattered at sea, as had been his wish. This prompted the wife to act accordingly, and she replied, "Yes, you're right, I agree with you. Let's do it now." With that she marched up to the bathroom with the urn clutched firmly in her hands, tipped the ashes into the toilet bowl and pushed the flush button. "He'll get there eventually," she said.

Friends and allies

The reason a lot of women get away with infidelity is that they have an ally in the form of a close girlfriend. It's so easy for a woman to say, "I'm going to meet Debbie after work, do some shopping and have a bit e to eat." Most men wouldn't bat an eye because it's the most natural thing for a woman to say. This is exactly what Anne did.

Debbie and Anne had been friends since high school, had similar lives and now, with their children growing up, these two best mates would occasionally go off on a girls' weekend together. It was on one such weekend that Anne met Tony. One thing led to another and they ended up embarking on an affair. Debbie and her husband owned a beach house close by but because of their busy schedule they never got to enjoy it. Debbie gave the key to Anne so she and Tony would have a private place to go to at lunchtimes. Sometimes, when Debbie's husband was out of town, she would let Anne use her house and Debbie would go out for an hour or so.

My experience shows that this kind of behavior is very common. The reason women can use a friend as an ally and get away with it is that women are natural communicator s. They talk on a deeper and more intimate level than men, sharing confidences and thoughts. Men are aware of this and don't think anything of it.

Who's the boss? Wives who blame the other woman and confront her

I've had so many clients do this, and I consider this behavior embarrassing and humiliating. It never seems to make the situation better; the wife never gets what she wants. In fact, on the whole, it seems to make matters worse because the lover either denies any involvement with the husband, which is incredibly frustrating, or she goes into so much detail it only causes more pain. Then the wife loses dignity in front of the other woman and in doing so gives her the power. So her plan has totally backfired, because the whole objective of the confrontation was to show her husband's lover who's the boss.

In many cases what usually happens after the confrontation is that the lover runs straight to the husband complaining about the verbal and sometimes physical abuse she has just endured and he takes her side against the wife. This only adds more fuel to the fire and makes the wife even more enraged. The vast majority of my clients blame the other woman for enticing their husband into infidelity, and believe he would never have crossed the line if he hadn't been seduced.

Dianna always had suspicions that something was amiss with her husband and she was usually right. On this occasion it was someone at his gym. There had been women in and out of her husband's life from day one of their 23-year marriage. Dianna had endured this behavior, believing it was the norm (all men cheat), but that way of thinking had never stopped her confronting the women in the past and it wasn't going to stop her now. Dianna truly believed her husband would never leave her, and in a sad sort of way she derived comfort from the fact that following her confrontation she always ended the affairs and stayed with her. And it was true that the only reason he ended the affairs was because she found him out, but it wasn't enough to stop him having affairs.

When we found out whom the other woman was Dianna was relentless in pursuing confrontation. She waited for her husband's lover outside the gym one evening, and then all hell broke loose:

> *You are nothing more than a cheap little tart and if you know what's good for you you'll leave my husband alone. He doesn't want you; you are just like all the other cheap little tarts that take their knickers off for him. If he loves you so much why is he still with me? I bet he tells you we don't have sex; that's what he told the last one but let me put you in the picture – we have plenty of sex.*

Dianna hadn't left the car park before his lover was on the phone to her husband giving him a piece of her mind because he'd told her he and Dianna slept in separate rooms. He spent the rest of the day comforting his lover, which only caused more devastation for his wife. Since then Dianna has shown up at the woman's work and harassed her on the phone – all in a misguided bid to show her she's the boss.

Key points

- When you marry you have a contract with your husband. When he betrays you and breaches the contract then he's the one at fault, not the other woman.

- Confrontation is always unbecoming. In doing so you are disrespecting yourself, and in your husband's mind that gives him justification to disrespect you further.

Boundaries

I find it fascinating how people's perceptions of betrayal differ. Bill Clinton had a very clear view that oral sex did not constitute betrayal because it wasn't penetration, and he's not alone, but many of my clients are vague when it comes to this. In the end it comes down to boundaries – what you will and will not accept as behavior conducive to a truthful and trustworthy relationship. If you put these boundaries in place prior to your marriage then there is no doubt and no misunderstanding in either of your minds that should these rules be broken, the injured party can act. A comparable example is that before you receive your driving license you sit a test, which means you understand the rules for driving your car. Failure to follow those rules when driving your car can have serious consequences, and this should be no different to the boundaries drawn up between two people entering into a relationship.

Very few couples actually discuss the nuts and bolts of what is really important to them before they get married. Despite the fact that this is supposed to be a lifetime partnership they are entering into, it appears that more discussion goes into the color of the flowers at the wedding than the boundaries they will accept. You might say, "I can't stand it when you fart in bed," but when it comes to the bigger issues, such as your views on infidelity, you are afraid that if you say what you really think you might not make it to the altar. This is incredible when you think about it, because we are talking about your life and future happiness. What better way to find out what his boundaries are than by observing his reaction when you raise the subject? At least when you do have the courage to sit down and discuss the details no one can say after the event, "I didn't know you felt that way, and I wouldn't have got involved if I had known. "At least this way you and your partner are under no illusions as to what you will and will not accept.

From a private investigator's point of view domestic peace-of mind work can be the most frustrating because most couples haven't addressed these issues. Therefore, if one or the other finds themselves having to deal with infidelity no amount of evidence is ever enough because the boundaries of the two parties are unknown. Just about every client wants to know that their partner has been caught in the act, yet for us to say that their partner has checked into a hotel room with another woman and spent the night with her is often not enough. They tell me that if they don't have actual proof, i.e. a photograph of sex taking place, then he will just lie, say nothing happened and accuse them of going mad. Well, of course he will. He's not about to say, "Yes, honey, I took my secretary out for a fantastic dinner, then back to my palatial hotel room for a night of rampant sex."

Forget about obtaining a photograph of the sex act. Instead, consider what he was doing with her in the first place. And if it's OK with you that your husband lies to you about what he's been doing, because clearly he has, you need to ask yourself, isn't the simple fact that your husband spent the night in a hotel room with another woman and never told you enough?

Key points

- Know in your mind exactly what behavior you will and will not accept from your partner.
- Make sure your partner has a clear understanding of your boundaries so that there is no confusion.
- If you do discover that your partner has lied to you and you are going to confront him, then you need to be prepared to act.

In the following cases it is interesting to note that all these women thought they were at fault for asking a question they had every right to ask. And what is even more interesting is that they were willing to accept whatever explanation their husbands gave. When I pointed out that to believe what their husbands had said could be a risk, in all cases there was stunned silence on the end of the phone, then they quickly sprang to their partners' defense by reiterating the explanations they had been given. Yet it is very simple. All of these women have proof that their partners have lied to them, so why are they willing to believe their partners' explanations?

In this book I'm going to keep repeating things over and over again until you get it: love is a behavior, not just a feeling. When a man lies to you he is consciously disrespecting you. When he tells you he loves you the words aren't enough. When a man lies to you his actions towards you are unloving. You can't gloss over it and make excuses-this is a fact. When women excuse their husbands' lies, whatever the lies are about, they are deluding themselves. As I've said before, there is nothing wrong with being compassionate and supportive but it's destructive to support excuses.

Take, for instance, Rebecca, whose husband Steve told her he was going on an office night out but never came home. He telephoned the following morning to say that he'd had too much to drink and had gone home with Mike and stayed at his place. This wasn't the first time he had stayed out all night after one of these "office bonding" sessions, but Rebecca had always believed his stories about why he hadn't returned. The nagging doubt that persisted for Rebecca was that he would only telephone the following morning, after the fact, and that it was only a 20-minute taxi ride home. This particular morning Rebecca decided to telephone Mike to see if the story stacked up, only to find a voice message saying Mike was out of the country and wouldn't be back for two weeks. When Rebecca questioned Steve about this he became aggressive and said, "I will not be interrogated by you. What is this, the Spanish Inquisition?"

Rebecca's reason for telephoning me was to ask if I thought she was overreacting as she had no evidence. But, in actual fact, she had all the evidence she needed. Marriage is a partnership based on respect and Rebecca knew Steve had lied to her. The only reason you lie is to cover up for something you have done. Steve had also become aggressive, which is another sign of guilt, and he could give no reasonable explanation for his behavior — because there wasn't one.

My response to Rebecca was to ask if lying was OK in her marriage, to which she replied, "Of course not." I cannot stress enough that couples need clearly defined boundaries relating to what is acceptable to both partners, and a universally held view is that lying in order to deceive is not acceptable. So what more proof do they want when they know their partner has lied to them?

Hannah and Chris had been married only three months when Chris started visiting his ex-girlfriend two or three times a week for what he claimed was coffee and a chat. Knowing that Chris had been very heavily involved with this woman before they met, Hannah didn't feel comfortable and asked Chris not to see her again. She explained to Chris that if she was just a female friend then an occasional coffee would be OK, but this woman had been his lover for many years and the closeness of their previous relationship left her feeling decidedly uncomfortable. Chris said he fully understood her concerns and promised he would have no further contact with his ex-girlfriend. A few weeks went by and Hannah was beginning to feel a little better, until one day she couldn't contact Chris on his cell phone and her anxieties came flooding back. So she drove by the ex-girlfriend's house and, sure enough, Chris's car was parked in her driveway. That night Hannah casually asked Chris if he'd heard from or spoken with this woman since he'd promised not to have contact, and he said, "No, I haven't seen her since we had our chat."

Hannah called me to ask if we could find out for her what was going on inside the house. I replied that we couldn't see through walls and she didn't need to know what was going on in the house because Chris was already showing a lack of respect by choosing to lie only two weeks after promising not to see his ex-girlfriend.

So once again the question of what your boundaries are and what you are willing to accept must be called into question. It's not a question of what other people are willing to accept, but what you personally are comfortable living with.

For some women the boundaries are stretched beyond any reasonable limit, so in essence they have no boundaries, and more importantly their partner knows this and uses it to continually abuse and disrespect them. Women who continually move the line in the sand further and further away show by their actions that they don't respect themselves either.

This is a common occurrence in my line of work, and is often apparent with couples in long-term marriages. They have been through counseling (usually at the wife's request) and now they are off to the lawyers (usually at the wife's request) where she is going to draw the very last line in the sand. Her husband is going to go along with this, just as he has before, because he knows that the tide always comes in to wash the line away.

Tina and Karl, whom I talked about in Chapter 4, "Women are their own worst enemies", are a prime example of a couple where the wife has lost all self-respect and her boundaries have stretched so far and wide that she can't remember where most of them are.

Tina and Karl are wealthy beyond most people's imagination, and splitting their matrimonial assets would leave them both in a position where they need never work again. So Tina decided she had drawn a line in the sand once too often and headed for the lawyer's office to get rid of Karl once and for all. As the lawyer drew up the various documents Karl used his trump card and in a show of emotion said he still wanted Tina and was so sorry for what he'd done that he wanted one last chance, and if she gave him this chance he would prove to her that he meant it. In front of the lawyer they both declared she wouldn't accept any further indiscretions and he would abide by his promise. Within days of that meeting Karl was back to his old tricks and to this day they are still together. Periodically they meet with lawyers to draw up more meaningless documents.

Male boundaries

I have thought long and hard about this particular facet of male behavior and I've come to the following conclusion, which seems to make sense (or at least it does to me).

Over the years I've been astounded at how many men take their lovers back to the matrimonial home, and more importantly into the matrimonial bed, with never a care or thought as to what this action means, not only to their marriage but to their wife. For men the home represents an asset, an investment, a status symbol or simply bricks and mortar, which means they have a far less emotional link with it than a woman would have. Men rarely describe the place they live in as their home, but as their house, their piece of real estate or their castle. The words used to describe it reinforce the lack of emotional attachment. Since time began women have had an intimate bond with their homes because it's where they have nurtured their families while their husband or mate hunted and gathered to supply their needs.

Because men don't share the same intimate bond with the home as women it's easier for them to betray there. Women, who have such a personal connection with their homes, wrongly assume their husbands do as well and would never consider betraying them at the heart of the family. When I've suggested such an occurrence may have happened or could happen I can hear the indignant tone in my clients' voices. They tell me their husbands would never take anyone back to the family home, but the truth of the matter is that this boundary is broken all too often.

> **In the previous chapter, I discussed women who thought it was less threatening to their marriage and position if their husbands visited prostitutes rather than had an affair. This thinking is based around their assumption that there is no emotional connection with a prostitute, and they are correct, but the flaw in this assumption is that men are suckers for a "damsel in distress". When men visit prostitutes they enter the realms of fantasy and often become the victims of a hard-luck story. This generally revolves around the girl needing money to get out of the industry, or needing cash to set herself up in her own flat so she can pursue her education or career. She may suggest she will be his special girl, and it would amaze you how many intelligent men allow themselves to be taken in by these women. You could say it's the "knight in shining armor" or Pretty Woman fantasy, but much nearer to the truth would be a lack of self-esteem and confidence on the part of the man, and this is borne out by the ease with which flattery works for these girls. That applies to most men who betray and covers all socio economic groups and job types. Remember, these**

girls wouldn't choose to be intimate with these men unless there was money involved. It's their job to make these men feel special. The girls are there for one reason and one reason only, and that is MONEY!

On a number of occasions we've been employed by men who have fallen into this trap. We've been asked to establish what their new found friend is up to in the apartment they have provided for her, and what educational courses she's attending. In all cases their new friend was making good use of the apartment, majoring in sex, and had far more than one special friend.

This is Jack's story.

The man on the other end of the phone had a friendly, cultured voice and introduced himself as Jack. He explained that he worked for a large city law firm and had been happily married for 27 years. My first response was to wonder why on earth this man was calling me. Until, that is, Jack said he'd fallen in love with another woman and was seriously considering leaving his wife for her. I suppose it's fair to give Jack credit for admitting to falling in love with another woman. And in his mind he was doing the honorable thing by ending his marriage. Then he told me the other woman was a girl he'd met at the massage parlor he frequented. Jack admitted he'd been helping her out financially as well as paying for her services, but he assured me it was only to help her get started out on her own because at the moment she lived

at home with her mother and baby brother. I gave Jack all the pearls of wisdom I had for a situation like this and wished him all the luck in the world because he would need it.

Obviously nothing I said sank in, because about two months later I got a call from a hospital. Jack was on the line, sounding very down in the dumps. The first thing he said was, "God, I wish I'd listened to you; I've totally blown it. You wouldn't believe what has happened."

Jack went on to say he'd put a bond down on an apartment and furnished it for the woman at the massage parlor, and he'd paid the deposit on a car, then he'd gone on a skiing holiday with his wife and family. Although he was going to tell his wife he was leaving her he couldn't ever find the right moment. However, during the skiing trip Jack suffered a terrible fall and shattered his leg, which put him in hospital and in traction for six months. He was beside himself with worry and wanted me to make sure his new love was coping at home alone. My investigators only had to watch for a day to find out that although Jack wasn't enjoying the fruits of the little love nest he had helped provide, other punters were.

Jack isn't the first and won't be the last to fall for the "damsel in distress" line, and he needn't have stressed himself too much as her new soft touch is an accountant who is sure to follow where Jack left off.

CHAPTER 6

Julia's story: Part 2

In 1974 people turned their noses up at women like me; I was only 21 but already I was divorced and had three young children, a young mother on her own. I was still a very naive young girl, but it didn't take me long to learn that no guy of my age was going to be emotionally or financially mature enough to take on an instant family. Needless to say I didn't have much money, but my parents helped me to ensure my kids were always beautifully turned out. Times weren't easy for them either. Mum was diagnosed with breast cancer and had a mastectomy. Dad's health wasn't too good either; he was diagnosed with prostate cancer.

I worked at any job I could to make ends meet, including fruit picking and modeling. I even went on welfare to make sure my kids and I could survive, but it was obvious to my parents and me that financially my little family wasn't going anywhere. But it's funny how life works sometimes. A few years later, when I was 27, a friend asked me if I was interested in some part-time secretarial work for the local branch of a major political party. I thought, why not? After all, you never know – I might meet some interesting people.

And I did. He was very powerful and charismatic, a man's man with a lot of equally powerful friends, and very rich – a multi-millionaire property developer. In his Dior suit, and dripping with diamonds and gold, he looked as if he'd stepped straight out of a gangster movie.

For some reason Mr. G was very interested in me – he made that plain very quickly when just a few days after we'd met he turned up on my doorstep. "Hi love, fancy a drive?" I looked over his shoulder at the huge new black saloon that was parked in my driveway. He was 18 years older than me and he spoke like a second-hand car dealer, but Mr. G had a way of getting people to like him. And for all his brashness he made me laugh. We had other things in common too. Our birthdays were only a day apart. He was a keen hunter, and so was I – after all, my family had been keen hunters as far back as I could remember. We had horses in common too, except they were part of his business; he bred and raced them. And most importantly, Mr. G wasn't fazed by the fact that I had three kids. My daughters in turn seemed to like him, too.

Even so, I could never have imagined that only two years later I would be selling my house and taking my daughters off to live on a beautiful 60-hectare farm, which Mr. G was developing into a huge stud facility for breeding racehorses. He poured millions into the local economy and from the outside it must have looked as if we had a fabulous lifestyle; rich and powerful moneymen came from round the world to do business with Mr. G, the man who owned the most expensive standard bred stallion in the country, Vance Hanover. And boy, did Mr. G know how to put on a show. We threw lavish parties with the highest-quality fresh fish and game meats, fine wines and entertainment. And at Mr. G's side was his glamorous, vivacious young wife – me.

But there was a side to those occasions the guests would never see: my side. One minute I was the hostess mingling with my guests, next thing I was back in the kitchen throwing on an apron and returning to my role as chief cook, dishwasher and cleaner. At one function alone I catered for over a hundred people, and I recall overhearing a conversation between two women who wondered what Mr. G's idle young wife did all day while he worked himself into the ground. Little did they know that the person who collected all their dirty dishes and washed them by hand was in fact me. The front we put up was just that:

a front. After the guests left, I was out the back cleaning the toilets.

Mr. G had a secret that even his closest friends didn't know about. The "life of the party" persona he wore in public hid a sometimes brutal man who was prone to black mood swings. He was controlling, a bully. He hit me. He told me what I could wear, right down to the shad e of nail polish. I remember him saying to me, "Don't wear red nail polish only sluts wear that!" At the start of each winter I had to wait until I was given permission to put an electric blanket on or activate the central heating.

I was constantly told that I didn't own a blade of grass on Mr. G's stud farm, and that he could kick me out "on my fat ass with nothing" anytime he chose. I learnt very early on to be subservient and not to cross him. He was the boss, and that was that. Mr. G had many secrets, many involvements and many connections that I cannot reveal in this book.

But in the late 1980s life changed hugely. Both my parents died from cancer, within 18 months of each other. It was devastating. They had been there for me all the way, despite how difficult it must have been for them. Then a couple of days after Mum died came the stock market crash of October 1987. Later I would be glad she didn't live to see what happened to us as a result.

The crash put Mr. G and his business under intense pressure; the clients were still lining up but the problem was that now they weren't paying. Mr. G and I

learned some big and painful lessons from people we had previously considered friends; at one stage we were owed almost a million dollars in unpaid service fees and charges by people who remain some of the biggest players in the industry. None of that money was ever paid, but those people know who they are and in my opinion they really don't deserve to be in the business.

I knew the end was near on the day a man in an immaculate dark suit pulled into our driveway in a new BMW. He was a company receiver who had come down from the big city to assess our business for a finance company we had a loan with. I can remember thinking he was a little overdressed for a man who had come to look over a stud farm, but of course we had gumboots so he wouldn't get his lovely shoes dirty. I had a beautiful lunch set out, which he duly demolished. We were then going to take him on a tour of the entire property but he was having none of that – no gumboots or overalls for him – just a walk around the buildings sticking to the paved areas, five minutes of questions and not a spot of mud on him. Then he roared off down the road back to the city.

About a month later, Mr. G's young wife received a letter asking her to attend a meeting with the receivers. Curious to see what this was all about; Mr. G had me dress in a manner befitting the wife of a millionaire stud-farm owner and duly drove me to the city. I walked into a room full of men, all seated around a table, who all looked like copies of the man who had visited us on the farm. It all started well enough; pleasantries flew thick and fast, but I do remember there was more than a little interest in the jewelry I was wearing. Then came the money question. You see, these men were convinced that Mr. G had squirreled away a very large amount of money in offshore bank accounts, and since his young wife appeared to have done a lot of overseas travelling in the preceding years, if anyone knew where the money was hidden it would be her. It was made clear to me that as Mr. G's wife I was duty bound to reveal all, and what's more, I was liable for any monies owing. The men were at pains to make clear there was a lot of money owing: "About $1.5 million, Mrs. G," I recall one of them saying pointedly.

There was a pause, and I remember them all looking at me as I said, "The thing is, you've got a bit of a problem ... because I'm not Mr. G's wife, you see; we're not married ..." You could have heard a pin drop. In those days the law was very different regarding de facto relationships; such unions had no standing in the eyes of the law, which meant that what Mr. G had told me was correct. I didn't own a blade of grass on his farm, but nor was I liable for any of his debts.

But soon after that things were to get worse, a lot worse. You see, I actually did have a little bit of money of my own, money from the sale of the house I'd owned when I first met Mr. G, and my inheritance from my parents' estate. That money had been invested in one of Mr. G's companies, where he assured me it was safe. For some years I had been receiving interest payment s, but suddenly these payments stopped. I started to get worried when each time I enquired about my money Mr. G fobbed me off with some excuse or other. After a while I knew something was seriously wrong, and I feared that if I didn't do something quickly I was going to lose everything I had left. I packed up all my mother's personal possessions and all my own and put them into storage. Mr. G thought I'd lost the plot, but luckily for me he was too preoccupied with his business problems to worry about what I was up to. I know now that if I hadn't done what I did all of my most treasured family possessions would have been sold off as part of Mr. G's chattels. Eventually Mr. G was forced to admit that he had been using my money, and that of friends who had also invested with him, to pay the running costs of the farm. I felt angry and betrayed, but I was so afraid of Mr. G's temper that there was no way I was going to argue it out with him; I just had to let it go.

By now the receivers had taken over the farm, and they were in a difficult position as they had no staff to run it. Each day we watched as yelling men in suits tried desperately to feed out to the animals from the back of an old truck in the pouring rain. Finally we had to move out, and just days before we had to leave a local farmer took pity on us and offered us an old house on his property where we could live temporarily. Trouble was, the farmer had been using the old house as his hay barn and it was full of moldy straw and rats. This was as low as Mr. G would ever go, and to have clawed his way to the top and then lost everything was devastating for him. We lived in that hay barn long enough to sort our affairs, sell whatever we could lay our hands on and plan our next move.

And it was a big move for all of us: my three children all moved out at that time and settled into jobs in the city. Mr. G and I scraped together what money we could find and left the country, bound for we didn't know what. Despite all the dramas we'd been through, I have to say the next 18 months were some of the happiest times of my life as we travelled rough around the world from South America to northern Europe. I was in my element; it was the best adventure I'd ever had. Every day there were amazing things to see and experience around every corner. And Mr. G and I had never been as close. There was calmness in our relationship — maybe it was because there were only two of us on this journey, maybe it was because we were finally on equal footing: both broke and vulnerable.

Whatever, somehow we ended up at Caesar's Palace with a marriage celebrant joining us together as man and wife. It was the day all the lights on Las Vegas' famed Strip were turned off for the first and only time in the city's history, when Sammy Davis jnr died. I remember I was saying "I do" when suddenly everything went black. This is not a good sign,"I thought."

At first, though, things were great. We spent a fantastic two years moving from country to country, eating delicious local food from roadside stalls and markets; some of the best meals I have ever eaten were some of the cheapest.

But Mr. G had no intention of living like this for long. He was a money-maker, a worker, and he had big plans to get back what he'd lost – sooner rather than later. So before too long there we were, back home, reunited with my children and all living in a large house in the country again (rented this time) as Mr. G pursued his latest business venture: pig farming.

It was wonderful to be back living with my girls again. They were really growing up – I got to see my oldest, Karoline, marry and have her first child; Louise followed suit, and shortly after Annika got married too. At 39 I was now a grandmother twice over!

But all the while, the stress of trying to rebuild his fortune was mounting for Mr. G. His black moods returned and I spent my time walking on eggshells so I wouldn't upset him. It was just like the bad old days back at the stud farm when he ruled with an iron fist. He had promised me when we got married that he would be a different man, that all the abuse, the controlling behavior, was a thing of the past. I was too young back then to know that a leopard never changes its spots.

Nothing I did ever seemed to be good enough. One night

I failed to take the bread out of the freezer for his dinner and he snapped: in a rage he grabbed the back of my head and slammed me into the floor, and then he rubbed his dirty socks in my face. My children looked on in horror and disbelief. Another time, Mr. G was so angry he just refused to talk to any of us for a whole week. Can you imagine what the atmosphere in that house was like? It was becoming so poisonous for all of us that something simply had to give, and it did the night Mr. G decided to pick a fight with Karoline's husband Shayne, a strapping 24-year-old who, like the rest of us, had had enough. Five minutes into a tirade about Shayne's character Mr. G suddenly found himself on the receiving end of a massive punch that left him lying on the floor in a pool of blood with a broken cheekbone. Shayne immediately rang the police and told them to bring an ambulance; they arrived with a howling of sirens 15 minutes later.

It was like something straight out of a TV cop show – lights flashing, and detectives and uniformed cops grilling us as we stood stunned, unable to believe what had just happened. "So what do you want to do, stay or go?" two young constables asked me as Mr. G was put in an ambulance. I was shaking, I could hardly think, but I knew this would be my only opportunity to get away from him, so I had to take it.

We all left that night and never went back. My kids soon dispersed to set up homes and lives for themselves, and four months later I was on an airplane heading for Europe trying to put as much distance as I could between me and Mr. G.

I'd spent 13 tumultuous years with Mr. G, and I have to admit that man probably taught me more than anybody else I have ever met. I learned that in life and business you had to trust your own instincts; that no matter how bad a hand you may be dealt, there is always a way you can pick yourself up and go on to bigger and better things. Most importantly, I had learned that I was a survivor. Mr. G's emotional abuse, the continual put-downs and the controlling behavior had only made me stronger and more determined to prove that I could stand alone and be successful.

There was no way I could have known that within weeks I would be working for one of the richest and most famous men in England, and that I had already met the man who was about to become husband number three.

> **Mr. G and I didn't talk again for seven years, until the same mutual friend who had first introduced us all those years ago when I had my brief foray into the political world decided that we should bury the hatchet. It's funny how life plays out sometimes, but I think there'd been too much history between us to leave things the way they were. I remember Mr. G was very nervous at first, but before too long it was like old times as we chatted away. In the years that we had been apart he had remarried and divorced, and subsequently we would occasionally meet up for coffee or dinner to reminisce about the good times. In 2007 he even asked me to marry him again, but that just wasn't going to happen. He admitted to having treated me terribly, but there was nothing he could do to change that, only assure me that he was now a different man. In 2008 Mr. G was reconciled with my children, including Karoline's husband Shayne, when he and I celebrated our birthdays together. For all of us, it was an acknowledgement that a chapter in our lives had finally been closed.**

CHAPTER 7

A word to the guys

What is it with you guys? Is it the lack of emotional maturity that has you measuring your manliness by the number of women you've had sex with? Or does it have something to do with low self-esteem and a lack of confidence? I know it's believed that members of the fairer sex are the ones who need constant attention, but men are like sponges when it comes to flattery. I think it's true to say that men believe in fairytales more than women do. They still believe girls are made from "sugar and spice and all things nice". Women are far more devious than men believe or ever give them credit for. Of course there are wonderful, warm, loving, caring women out there looking for Mr. Wonderful. However, that's "Mr. Single Wonderful" not "Mr. Married with Kids".

The women who don't fit that category come with varying degrees of danger attached. Some are demanding, controlling, manipulative, greedy, mercenary and sheer bloody ruthless – but with enough sugar coating to disguise the fact. Then there are the ones who appear to be coy, feeble, vulnerable and helpless – the "I've never had a good relationship with anyone until you came along" kind of gal – and this is the one who appeals to the "knight in shining armor" kinda guy. Finally, there are the ones who are a little more obvious and come with drinking problems, are physically and verbally abusive and can be irrational and extremely volatile, and yet because these women will say they love you, you can't possibly reject them. She wants you. She really wants you!

The male need for female approval is a major concern. Why is it men feel that if the bus stops here they have to get on, and without thinking of the consequences? The key to avoiding getting on the wrong bus, or any bus if you're married, is to ask yourself why you're at the bus stop in the first place. What do you want? What do you need? And what have you already got? A truly confident man already knows how incredibly special and unique he is. That doesn't mean he can't enjoy a compliment; it just means that when some stunning female pays him some attention he's emotionally mature enough to acknowledge it without his ego getting in the way and jeopardizing everything he has.

For all those philanderers out there

What I find so incredible about this whole issue of infidelity is that there's a bunch of you out there who meet, find attractive and finally fall in love with women, have children with them and then, without any regard for the family they helped to create, go about making their lives a misery through your selfishness and total lack of respect. You've made choices, and now you have to man-up and accept the responsibilities that come with those choices, and the devastating effects they have on your family's lives. It's not all about you.

The two most overused responses men offer when confronted with their infidelity are "She was just someone I could talk to because we were having problems" and "I just need to move out for a few months so I can sort myself out".

Yeah, right, that makes a whole lot of sense. It's really helpful to rebuild your relationship with your wife by having sex with someone else, and it makes even more sense to try to fix your relationship when you've removed yourself from it. And then you honestly wonder why you can't seem to get that old level of intimacy back and those feelings of love. You'll say, "How can I when this woman is always on my case? She's prying into my every move and constantly rehashing the past at every opportunity."

What will it take before you guys get it? Remaining faithful is all that's required, and that means being devoted, dependable, reliable, constant and truthful. How hard is that? There is no other magic ingredient to a successful, happy relationship full of fun, love and passion. When a woman knows in her heart that she's the one, the only one, and she feels she can fully trust her man then the flames of passion burn bright. And boys, you don't know what you're missing, because it's a fact that women become more sexual and passionate as the years go by. Surely you haven't forgotten how fantastic your life together was in the beginning? That's because you made a promise to be faithful and she believed you, but once you breached that promise in essence you waived your rights. The chances of getting back what you had are slight at best and non-existent if you ever repeat the offence.

For all those philanderers out there who truly want to make their relationships work, the answer doesn't lie in how successful you perceive yourself to be; how others see you; how financially well off you are; how intelligent you are or what education you have – it has everything to do with your level of emotional maturity and integrity. The majority of my clients' husbands range from their late thirties to their fifties, but they display the emotional maturity of five-year-old s – "I want what I want when I want it and I want it now."

There is nothing more unattractive to a woman than an emotionally immature man. In fact, real men don't behave in this manner. If you know in your heart that you can't handle temptation without wanting to take it one step further (and this type of behavior doesn't just sneak up on you overnight; you know as well as I do that you've been like this all your adult life) then what you need to do is be man enough to stand up and take responsibility. Either leave or clean up your act once and for all. You don't have the right to ruin the lives of those around you, i.e. your wife and family.

I have a simple question to ask. If you look at all your indiscretions (probably meaningless ones in your mind) would you have done any of them with your wife standing next to you? You know the answer as well as I do, so don't try to minimize the degree of immaturity in the choices you have made.

Then there's the message you're sending to your children, because behavior like this is usually learnt. Is this how you would want your sons to behave? Would you want a man who treats women with the same disrespect as you do to marry your daughter? If not, think about the message you're sending. Daughters see their fathers as role models for men. Are you a man of integrity?

Let me tell you something that I absolutely know for sure – how to measure your success as a man. It's when your words and your actions match. It's when you have the integrity to do the right thing when no one else is watching. If you take nothing else from this book, take this.

The ground rules for an honest and committed relationship are simple: the proof is in the evidence. She's not interested in what you say; she's only interested in what you do. This means no secrecy and no lies. If you've had your mobile phone bill, your credit card accounts and your bank statements moved from home to your office send them home again. The only way to prove you have nothing to hide is by hiding nothing. Leave your briefcase unlocked, take the pin number off your phone, remove the password from the computer; you have to be an open book and become transparent. This is the only way you'll have any hope of retrieving your relationship. If you can't or won't do these things then she'll never ever be able to get over your infidelity – and I mean never. Whatever you do, don't underestimate the damage that is done by your infidelity and lying. Remember, boys – girls are wired differently, and when you betray us it penetrates right to the core of our emotional being. We are nurturers and protectors. Dishonesty is like a virus. Once it invades our systems then we automatically try to destroy that virus and expel it from our lives. The greater the deceit the harder it will be for you to regain the trust and dig yourself out of the hole. It won't happen overnight, but it may happen. The choice is yours.

Let's talk about control

I know a lot of you guys don't see yourselves as control freaks but many of you are, whether you're willing to admit it or not. There's no need for the wife to be bothered with the mundane matter of money, right? Wrong. This isn't 1950, when it was accepted that the man handled the finances and the little wife kept the home and dared not question her husband. Women today do want a say in the family finances. After all, it's supposed to be an equal partnership you've entered into. If you keep investments, stocks, bank accounts, trusts and mortgages to yourself and are under the illusion that you can do what you want with the joint assets (and that's what they are) then that is called control.

Too often I come across women who are the wives or partners of men like you. Men who control the family finances purely and simply to fund their infidelities, and then live under the illusion that as long as their wives are well taken care of they'll have no grounds for complaint.

You might think this will give you free rein, but let me tell you that when you continue to control in this way, in the long run it will effectively work against you. Your wife didn't enter into a relationship to go backwards, but under this amount of control that is exactly what she's doing. Our parents controlled us for our own good but then we matured and in most cases left that control and went out on our own. Think about it this way: do you want your wife to see you as her father? Too much of this and she's going to leave your control, or maybe turn the tables on you.

You can try to convince yourself that what you're doing is for her own good, but that's bullshit. If it was for her own good, why all the secrecy?. We both know the reason for that: "When you've got nothing to hide you hide nothing."

If you are spending joint funds on another woman or women then stop and think – whose money is it? Half of it belongs to your wife or partner, and you can bet all the tea in China that if she knew what you were doing with it then it wouldn't be happening. The ultimate test is to ask yourself the next time you are siphoning off funds or setting up another trust in which your spouse or partner isn't involved – would you do it if she knew what the consequences were for her long-term future?

The biggest catalyst that leads a wife or partner to seek legal advice isn't financial betrayal but emotional betrayal, and the uncovering of one leads more often than not to the uncovering of the other, so keep in mind that the day of reckoning is never far away.

The link between porn and infidelity

Let's make something perfectly clear from the start: I'm no prude. If I were I wouldn't have lasted five minutes in this job, because there are times when it feels as if I am literally working in the sex industry. And the evidence shows a common thread that runs through certain dysfunctional relationships – pornography and infidelity. The two go hand in hand.

Now I'm going to share with you something else that I absolutely know for sure. Again, I know this purely and simply because of the overwhelming amount of evidence I've seen over the years. Many of the women I work for (your wives, girlfriends or partners) seek my advice because they think there must be something wrong with them sexually. Some are being pressured into sexual situations that are not to their liking, while others find themselves living in sexless relationships. This is because you're so caught up in playing out your fantasies and visiting prostitutes that you lose the ability to function in the real world with real women – i.e. your wives, girlfriends or partner s.

As I've said, this makes it impossible for your wives, girlfriends or partners to live up to your fantasies, so over time you turn off from what's real and live with what's not. These women are torn between their love for you, and wanting to please you, and their own sense of self-preservation. The reason they feel this way is that they're not comfortable with some of your sexual desires and demands.

I've lost count of the complaints I hear from women who tell me they've gone along with sexual activities because of the pressure brought to bear by you. They wouldn't normally consider these activities but they do so in order to fulfill your fantasies and desires, only to feel sick, humiliated and degraded. Often they attempt to be more accommodating so you don't stray again. They don't want you to come down on them with the old guilt trip: "Well, honey, if you would only be more sexually adventurous I wouldn't need to go looking for it." (Oh, please – get a grip!) There are lots of women who will try almost anything to keep their man, no matter how humiliating. When they refuse to participate, they're made to feel unloving and inadequate as women.

The activities you want them to participate in range from group sex to watching you have sex with both women and men, or maybe you want to watch your wife have sex with another woman. You'll have come up with various reasons for wanting this behavior, the biggest crock being how it will bring the two of you closer together. Having disconnected sex for sexual gratification alone doesn't enhance a loving, intimate relationship, especially when it's performed under duress.

You guys are incredibly transparent, not only to me but to the women in your lives. However, they're afraid or unsure how to confront this issue, and what I usually tell them is this: it's like someone asking you to do something that isn't sexual or illegal but wrong in your eyes. You have every right to decline. It's your right to live the life you want. It has nothing to do with what anyone else says is normal, and has everything to do with what you feel is right. And that's what counts.

Men who put the pressure on and try to manipulate and control through sex are usually inadequate, and incapable of true emotional intimacy and trust. The same goes for guys who frequent prostitutes and spend hours in porn sites and chat rooms on the internet. This is escapism, a quick fix for an ongoing problem. Guys who participate in these forms of sexual gratification feel fantastic, acceptable and masculine without ever deserving to feel this way. But it never ends there, and that's where I come in.

So as much as you try to justify it — it's harmless fun, or you're only looking — when will you get the message that women don't want men who are constantly looking at, wanting or having other women?

What it is that women want?

Let me tell you what women are really looking for: a man who is confident in himself and desires only one woman — THEM!

The more you show the woman in your life that you desire variety and that she's just not enough woman for a man like you, the further you push her out of your heart. Thank God there are real men out there, men who have got it. They have everything you want and crave. They have variety and excitement; fantastic, fulfilling, mind-blowing sex, combined with passion, admiration, love, respect and commitment — and all with just one woman.

"My God, how can that be possible?" you ask. Well, firstly they grew up and learnt a few simple rights from wrongs. They developed emotional maturity instead of being emotional cowards. They aren't on a quest for external fulfillment because they've realized that self-worth is far more important than an over-inflated ego (the downfall of many a man). They're happy in the knowledge that actions speak louder than words. But more importantly, they learnt long ago that you get out of your relationships what you put in. And believe me when I say there is nothing more desirable and sexy to a healthy and intelligent woman than an emotionally mature, confident man of integrity.

CHAPTER 8

Men are their own worst enemies

Facing the truth

I find men and women to be quite different in their approach to hiring a private investigator. When they talk to me, men invariably give me the third degree: they want to know who I am, what my qualifications are, and so on.

Here's an extreme example: I once had an Iranian client whose Spanish wife was having an affair with a Frenchman. The Iranian husband insisted that if he was going to discuss the case with me there had to be a male present. When I did meet him (with a male investigator in tow) he grilled me extensively on my abilities and background and then spent most of the ensuing meeting apologizing to me for the fact that he had to have a male present .

Men also need to have tangible proof that an affair is taking place before they will believe it. But once they do believe their partner is cheating they are much more likely to end the relationship forthwith, unlike women, who will usually give their cheating partner more chances to modify their behavior.

Client: "Hi, Julia, my name's Bob and I need your help and advice. Can you tell me if my wife is having an affair?"

Julia: "Well, Bob, you obviously think something is up, so tell me why you feel that way."

Client: "OK, I've been with my partner for about ten years, and three months ago she moved out because she said she needed space and now she's flatting with this guy."

Julia: "Who is this guy?"

Client: "Oh, he's a friend of hers I've never met, but she says they're just good friends and nothing's going on."

Julia: "Had she ever mentioned this friend prior to leaving?"

Client: "No."

Julia: "Before she left, did you notice any changes in her behavior?"

Client: "Oh yeah, she started taking really good care of herself and buying all this new underwear and our sex life came to a screeching halt."

Julia: "Did the two of you try to resolve any of your problems? Have you had any counseling?"

Client: "I wanted to have counseling, but when I suggested it she didn't want to know and kept saying she just needed space. I never even knew where she was living until a week ago when my daughter told me, and she also told me that sometimes Mummy lies on Graham's bed, but my partner denies everything and I know she wouldn't lie to me. You know, this is killing me because recently she had to have an operation and I went to visit her in the hospital, then later in the day I called back to see her and there was this guy there holding her hand, but when I questioned her later she said he was just trying to keep her awake. Can you tell me if they're having sex? I need to know."

Julia: "Bob, let's look at this picture so far. You've been in a relationship for ten years and you have a daughter with your partner. She leaves you and moves in with a man she says is a friend, but you've never met this friend. She doesn't tell you where she is living, and if your daughter hadn't told you I wonder how long it would have been before you found out. She says she needs space, so that's not saying the relationship is over yet. But she doesn't want to do anything to resolve any issues between the two of you. All this information is telling me that your partner has something to hide. If this man is just a friend, why haven't you met him? After all, he's the male figure around your daughter at the moment; therefore you have a right to know who and what he is. You only found out by chance where your partner and daughter are living, and if it is so innocent you should have known from the start. If she needs space one can only presume it's to sort herself out, but then she should be living on her own and actively working on herself , i.e., getting some professional help, which doesn't seem to be happening."

There is a long silence before the conversation starts again and Bob reveals that his partner and her new friend often go out together at the weekends and on occasion have even gone away together. In essence they're acting very much like a couple but all the time insisting all is above board. All the while Bob is making excuses for his partner. He will explain a situation to me, ask for my opinion, and then tell me I'm wrong because his partner's not like that. Every time I answer one of Bob's questions, using all my years of experience, he keeps trying to convince himself he's right by telling me how wrong I am and how his partner would never do half of the things he's previously told me she has done.

Are you confused? Well, I am. By the time we end the conversation Bob seems pretty mad at me for telling him the truth as I see it. If someone had told Bob this story I'm sure he would have had a very different view from the one he currently has. But human nature is such that because betrayal is so painful we will do everything to try to block it out, even when we know it's happening.

Bob's case is not an isolated one and brings to mind

another case, that of a guy I call "the apologist" (so much so that this man should have been running his partner's PR campaign).

Chris has actually been a long-standing client, and he has been involved with Charlene for eight years. The reason for his most recent call was that he found a text message from another man on her phone, and now he fears losing Charlene because he hasn't married her.

They don't live together, and in fact reside in separate towns many hundreds of miles apart, but they have a number of joint assets. Chris is 15 years older than Charlene and is totally besotted with her, yet they've had problems pretty much from day one. The main issue according to Charlene is that Chris hasn't married her, but from his point of view it isn't for the want of trying.

Since his very first phone call to me Chris has related a sorry tale of failed proposals of marriage. Two years into their relationship and on a trip back from Italy Chris produced a two-carat diamond ring and proposed to Charlene while they were sipping champagne in First Class. That was Chris's first mistake. Charlene said that an airplane was an inappropriate place to propose, and why hadn't he done it on the beach in Sorrento?

As time went by Charlene started to wear the ring and so Chris, his hopes raised, asked her where she would like him to propose to her. Her answer was: "Use your imagination; somewhere romantic." So Chris whisked Charlene away to the Bahamas, and as the holiday progressed she appeared to relax. Feeling that she would be receptive to a proposal, Chris decided now was the time.

Chris made his second mistake when he felt he could kill two birds with one stone, by not only proposing but also marrying her while they were on holiday. But Charlene was having none of his proposal or wedding, pointing out to him that for her to get married she would need the right dress, all the trimmings, with a hundred guests. She didn't want to get married on some beach somewhere far from home and her friends and family. From that moment on the holiday was over. Charlene constantly reminded Chris of his failure to get the proposal right, and then took the first available flight home, leaving him to ponder his future.

The relationship continued to deteriorate due to Chris's inability (in Charlene's eyes) to get something as simple as a proposal right. As I listened to this I was thinking that most girls would wish for even half Charlene's luck. But everyone's different and Charlene knew just how to play Chris. She had the best of both worlds, with Chris supporting her financially while she retained the freedom to come and go as she pleased.

As the relationship deteriorated further Chris became more concerned about Charlene's attitude to his coming to stay as often as he used to. In fact, she was becoming downright rude about it. But through all of this Chris was blaming himself for not finding the right place and time to propose, when what was really happening was that she was beginning to withdraw from him, even though she still continued to say that everything would be all right once he married her.

During one of our many phone conversations I asked Chris to describe Charlene to me. He outlined all her physical attributes and told me how beautiful she was and how much he loved her, and went on to say that though she could have very black moods and does have problems these were brought on because he hadn't married her. Nothing I said seemed to have any effect. He kept repeating how everything was his fault and how smart, intelligent, witty and charming she could be, and what a fantastic personality she had when they were out, how everyone loved her (but no one knew her like he did), and if it wasn't for her black moods and cutting tongue everything would be fine.

I tried and tried to explain to this man that she didn't want to marry him, because if you love someone it doesn't matter where they propose to you – you're not marrying the proposal, you're marrying the person. Even if Chris went to live with Charlene I would give him a week before there was another problem and it would all be his fault. I explained that he needed to take responsibility for his part in the relationship, because as long as he continued to take on the guilt Charlene loaded on him she'd keep on using that as a tool to control the relationship and keep it the way she wanted it.

This entire situation boils down to the fact that Chris is very insecure. He feels that if he takes back his power and the relationship finishes he will never get anybody as sexy and fantastic as Charlene. Chris is a man living in fear, refusing to face the facts, and in doing so will continue to suffer the consequences.

This is a very common pattern that I see in both men and women, and I call it the "but" syndrome. My clients describe their partners in glowing terms, as Chris did: "She's beautiful, sexy, and gorgeous and the most amazing woman I've ever met but ..."Or a woman might say about her husband: "He's a wonderful father, husband and provider. He's so good-looking and we have so much in common, but..."

What these people don't realize is that it's the word "but" that stops these relationships progressing.

When men are betrayed

Ask any man and he will tell you that women talk far more than men do. I disagree. Go into any bar and watch men talking about sport – the din is deafening. They can strike up a conversation with a perfect stranger and talk for hours. What men mean when they say that women talk more is not that we actually talk more, but that we talk about different things. Men find it unsettling that women can launch into quite private areas of their lives without a backward glance, and yet in my business it's men who volunteer so much graphic detail regarding their partners' personal habits, such as stains and smells on underwear. The average person wouldn't imagine a man would go into such detailed descriptions (as this is seen as the female domain) nor would they expect men to want these articles of clothing to be forensically tested.

Men phone me because it's easier to discuss vaginal secretions with a female than with some big burly ex-cop, but then they challenge me about my credentials. Knowing I'm not ex-police, they want a full report on my back ground and qualifications for doing the job. In other words, do I have a degree in snooping?

I'll never forget the look on the face of one of my male investigators when we were out on a case and I got a call in my car. The call came through over the speaker, and this guy launched into a description of how much discharge he saw each night in his wife's underwear. He was convinced she was having an affair with someone at her work. As my investigator sat listening to this he looked as if he was in considerable pain. When the call ended he said, "You have got to be kidding me. Does everybody tell you stuff like that?" I replied, "No, only men."

The reason for these graphic descriptions is that men don't use their intuition; therefore the evidence has to be something tangible. They approach infidelity in a practical manner and miss the subtle warning signs women are often attuned to. Men become far more desperate and obsessive when it comes to their partner's infidelity. To them it's a sign of their own weakness. Their masculinity and ego are under threat. "How dare she look for another mate when I'm so desirable?"

A noticeable aspect of men dealing with infidelity is that when they do come to me they can be wrong or they may have left it too late. I've said many times that when clients come to me for advice they are 100 per cent right, but I need to clarify here that I'm talking about my female clients. Because men don't take enough notice of their wives and their daily routines, they will often misread the signs they do pick up on.

> **Trevor had us follow his wife after finding a garter belt in her underwear drawer that he hadn't seen before. He was convinced she was up to no good in her lunch hour because whenever he asked to meet her she said she was too busy. We followed Trevor's wife as she went window shopping, and we found there was one shop she purchased from**

regularly, and that was the haberdashery store, where she bought elastic, lace and ribbon.

We informed Trevor that based on our experience, which came from observing so many people deceiving their partners; his wife wasn't playing around on him. We concluded she was making garter belts. But by this stage Trevor was totally obsessed and irrational, to the point where it was difficult dealing with him. As it turned out we were absolutely correct. His wife had been making garter belts for a friend who held "naughty knickers" parties. Had Trevor actually listened to his wife he would have known this, and if he'd added to this the fact that he'd never had cause for concern before, he would have saved himself a lot of anxiety and stress.

CHAPTER 9

When you live with a liar

When you live with a liar there are certain behavioral traits you may encounter – most significantly, the will to deceive. Whether the lie is blatant or a lie by omission, the intention is the same. It is a conscious and deliberate act to conceal or misrepresent the truth to keep you from knowing the facts.

Lying in a relationship will erode it over time, and there is nothing more destructive to your health and well-being than living with a liar. There are so many ways in which people can lie, and those men who lie will try to rationalize, minimize and justify their behavior when caught out. They may offer up one or many of the following excuses:

- I had good reason.
- I didn't want to hurt you.
- I didn't mean to.
- It just happened.
- I was drunk.

Women, on the other hand, will often rationalize, minimize and justify their partners' lying to avoid dealing with the truth. This may take one of the following forms:

- Well, he's only human after all.
- I know he didn't want to hurt me.
- It's probably my fault; I've put on weight.

Then there is the transferring of guilt. He may say something like:

- You make me feel like you don't care anymore.
- Oh, well, you accused me of having an affair so I thought I might as well have one.
- If only you'd looked after yourself better it wouldn't have happened.

So what do women do? They take the guilt on board and start believing they've driven their husband into the arms of another woman because they're too fat, too thin, too tall, too short, too old, not exciting enough – the list is endless. Men will always try to get themselves off the hook by making it their partner's fault. Don't get caught up in the blame game. Remember, there is no excuse for his lying to you. You can't make him lie to you – lying was his choice and his decision.

The artful dodger is the guy who appears to be going to take responsibility for his actions but then in mid-flight changes gear and tries to shift the blame onto the other woman.

In Pete's case it all started with a lipstick stain on a pristine white business shirt. When Pete arrived home the first thing his wife noticed was the lipstick stain on the inside of his shirt collar. Pete had to come clean and confess all, but instead of taking responsibility he made it out to be the woman's fault. He explained to his wife that when he'd returned to the office to pick up some papers one of the women was just about to leave and they got chatting. Then out of the blue she took off her blouse and unbuttoned my shirt and took it off and started kissing me. She was making all the moves but nothing happened. I didn't even fancy her. I've said I'm sorry. What more do you want?

If your husband has betrayed you and has been backed into a corner then he's probably had to acknowledge that he's cheated on you. This acknowledgement comes complete with protestations such as: "I'm sorry, it will never happen again," or "I'll prove to you that you can trust me," and he will usually feel after such an apology that he's vindicated and you should give him credit for his confession.

Jack was a master at lying and cheating and apologizing and confessing but when caught he was never able to deliver on any of his promises. Once jack had made an apology, in his mind the matter was closed.

Two weeks after being caught in his latest infidelity, and his sub sequent confession, Jack and his wife were watching a television program in which the husband was caught cheating on his wife. Jack looked across at his wife and there were tears in her eyes, because any reminder of her own situation was emotional torment and after only two weeks her wounds were fresh.

Jack asked her, "What's the matter with you?"

She replied, "I'll give you three guesses," to which Jack responded, "Oh, no, not that again. I thought you were over it."

Jack's wife asked me what she should do about his attitude and this is what I told her. This isn't about what Jack says. It's about what Jack needs to do and what is non-negotiable in your relationship in order to make progress. Your role is to have a list of requirements and not to back down no matter how heartfelt his words may be. This is about actions. It's about Jack taking responsibility and actively working on changing his behavior so that in the future he makes healthy choices.

When a grown man who's never shed a tear in his life suddenly bursts into tears when confronted with his lies, beware, because he may very well be playing on your sympathy. Watch out for phrases such as:

- I feel so bad about this.
- OK, so I lied, but I didn't kill anyone.
- You know I love you and would do anything for you.

- My actions make me so depressed I feel like killing myself.

These pathetic responses need dealing with in a firm way. Let him know quite clearly you are aware he's upset but that you've been more than upset by his lies, and if he doesn't respond to your needs there can be no way forward.

Danger! Danger!

This is the worst man you may have the misfortune to encounter. He is dangerous, blatant, single-minded, self-centered, egotistical and extremely persuasive. There aren't enough words to describe a man like this other than to say he comes across as charming, understanding, sensitive, romantic and exciting and is often a good lover, but there is a vital part of him missing. He is incapable of love – feeling it or giving it. Although he may say "I love you," even this is a lie because his actions towards you will be anything but loving. He simply doesn't have the components required and there is nothing you can do to change this man.

He is incapable of any depth of feeling because he is a sociopath. Through my work I've met a number of these men. They are the men who do the most damage, and the dreadful reality is that no amount of counseling and therapy will have any effect – I'm sure many psychologists will agree with me on this one. It's a waste of time punishing a sociopath; they never learn from experience, as there is always another victim around the corner. There may be windows of hope when he appears to see the error of his ways but there's nothing anyone can do to prevent this man reverting to type.

Alice met a sociopath and four years on she still bears

the scars. Charles was a highly respected man amongst his peers, but no one really knew much about his private life and certainly not his dark side. Alice met Charles at a conference they were both attending. He was charming and attentive and this led to an intense few days together. Alice was totally swept off her feet. She couldn't believe she'd met a man who was so sensitive, listened to what she had to say and certainly looked the part. But Charles was playing a role, and this behavior had nothing to do with who Charles really was.

The sociopath is like a chameleon; they change their persona to suit the environment and situation. Charles worked his charm and in a very short time had convinced Alice to leave her husband and children. She moved into a house and waited for Charles to leave his wife and join her as promised. But Charles had no intention of living with Alice, or Christine or Janet, all of whom were waiting for him. Two of these women confronted his wife, but so plausible was the story he told her that she totally believed him and is still with him today. All three of the other women are still trying to piece together their broken lives.

The best way to get over a romantic encounter with a sociopath is to make an appointment with a psychologist to gain an understanding of how these people operate. This will be the first step in moving forward.

CHAPTER 10

Julia's story: Part 3

"You are Harrods, Miss Moore – you are exactly the sort of person we are looking for here." I had at lived in London virtually penniless, to be referred within days to Europe's most famous luxury department store for my first and, as it turned out, only English job interview. It was a match made in heaven as far as I was concerned, a fact that was confirmed when Harrods hired me to work in their perfumerie.

Harrods has been synonymous with luxury, glamour and excess for over 150 years. It is frequented by royalty and Hollywood stars alike, and is one of England's top tourist destinations. It used to be said that if you couldn't buy it at Harrods, you couldn't buy it anywhere – exemplified by the story of the man who walked into Harrods' exotic animals department in the 1960s and asked to buy a camel. "Certainly, Sir," said the unflappable sales assistant; "One hump or two?"

Only a matter of hours into my first day behind the counter I heard a familiar voice say, "What on earth are you doing here?" You can imagine how gob smacked I was when I turned around to find a familiar face grinning at me. I'd met Andrew a year earlier while ferrying racehorses from New Zealand to Hong Kong for Mr. G. He was English, tall, good-looking and charming, with a real silver tongue, and now he was standing in front of me asking me out to lunch. "Well, why not?" I thought. "I don't know anybody else here, and it can't do any harm."

My first months in London were a blur as lunch dates with Andrew became dinner dates and then much more. After spending 13 years with a man who was almost 20 years older than me, Andrew was a breath of fresh air. We were the same age for starters; he was fit, young, and I found him wildly interesting. We were soon inseparable, and before I knew it we were living together. Looking back now I can see how damaged, how vulnerable I was at that time, and Andrew was the last kind of man I should have been getting involved with, because he was also damaged. It was the old story – like attracts like – but I had yet to find out just what kind of man Andrew really was.

My days were long – up at 5.30 to catch the bus into London, and flopping back into bed exhausted each night, only to do it all again the next day, and the next. But I loved my job. You never knew who you might run into in the course of a day – people like Rod Stewart, George Hamilton, Pierce Brosnan – they were all as you'd expect, charming and engaging to a fault. Princess Diana was as beautiful and warm as they say, a real stunner.

But not everybody was such a pleasure to deal with. There was the man who demanded: "I want to buy all of your products ... how much for everything ... and you?" He was a Nigerian prince, clad in full royal regalia including a robe and feathered turban. He was determined to buy me, and if I would go with him he would buy up the shop's entire male grooming section. He made it very clear that he wasn't going to take no for an answer, and it took a forceful intervention by the head of Harrods security, a very nice gentleman by the name of Steve, to convince him that no, the lady wasn't for sale under any circumstances. The prince and his entourage swept out of the store indignantly, bemoaning the standard of service and loudly proclaiming they would never return under any circumstances.

Then there was the small matter of my relationship with Mr. Harrods himself, Mohammed al Fayed. I was standing by the lifts one morning looking for a suitable candidate on whom to test a new designer perfume for men. "Would Sir like to try the new fragrance by Davidoff?" I volunteered as I moved in to spray a small, dapper man who had seemingly emerged from nowhere. Before my finger could even touch the spray button I was surrounded by tall men in dark suits, one of whom warned me to keep my distance from the boss, Mr. Mohammed al Fayed.

There was a warm chuckle and I turned around to see Mr. Fayed smiling at me and asking my name. "Miss Moore, it is a real pleasure to meet someone who is so enthusiastic about their work here," he said. I can't claim to have got to know him well, but I think Mr. Fayed liked me as he remembered my name and we had regular chats when he made his daily inspections of the store.

But Mr. Fayed would have been very angry if he'd overheard the same conversation that I heard in the ladies' powder rooms a few days later, one morning before the store opened for business. I was in a cubicle when I heard a group of young women come in and start talking animatedly. Their accents seemed to be Scottish and Irish, and they were discussing the types of luxury product they were smuggling out of the store, including how much and just how they were doing it. I couldn't believe what I was hearing, and was in a real dilemma as to whether I should stay put until they left or just walk out and pretend I hadn't heard anything unusual. Well, I decided to just walk out. "Hey, Julia," smiled a young woman, who was standing with a group of about half a dozen others. She was a very pretty girl whom I knew rather well. I said hello and kept on walking.

The next morning before work the same girl approached me again. "If there's anything you want, I can show you how to get it out of the store," she told me bluntly. Harrods, as all its 5000 staff were aware, was losing tens of thousands of pounds a month to theft, the majority of it employee theft. Well, I talked to this girl for some time, and what she told me was shocking. It turned out her group was smuggling out a huge amount of stolen goods every day under the noses of the security staff. They'd noticed my familiarity with management and their message was clear: join them in their scam, or else.

This put me in a very difficult situation, but luckily I had become friendly with someone I could talk to about it all, a lovely English girl who was in charge of all the counter staff. She was as horrified as I was and said we had to do something about it; after all, as she pointed out, I had signed a legal contract with Harrods that obliged me to act. She asked if she could have my permission to tell security what was going on. Well, unfortunately I am legally constrained from telling you much more, but suffice to say that after a few months of drama the head of security came up to me and said, "Miss Moore, you have the makings of a first-class detective."

While I was doing well at Harrods, at home things seemed to be ticking along nicely too. Andrew and I did plenty of travelling to Europe and within England, including a trip to Bristol where we stayed at the house of a friend of Andrew's while she was away skiing in Switzerland. It wasn't until much later that I realized the truth behind our stay there. At the time I was very impressed with how dedicated Andrew was to his teenage sons, who were from a previous marriage; every second weekend he made a point of travelling up to Yorkshire to spend time with them. I would spend those weekends alone at our flat outside London, reading or watching TV. I remember getting hooked on a British series about two female private eyes, Chandler and Co, and thinking, "You know, I could do that!" But while I didn't mind being left alone I started to become very homesick. The truth was I missed my three daughters terribly.

A year had passed since my arrival in England and I was tired, weary of the daily grind of life in London, and I guess I had reached the point where I just wanted a more substantial life. I made the decision to give my notice at Harrods, then I packed up my things, said farewell to Andrew and boarded a plane bound for home.

I had been well paid by Harrods and had saved enough money for a deposit on a small beachside cottage outside Auckland. My friends thought I was mad — they thought I'd bought a run-down dump — but to me it was beautiful, rustic and, most importantly, it was all mine. I had enough money left over, along with a quantity of jewelery, to satisfy the bank and to service the mortgage for a year, but it was clear that I was going to have to come up with a more permanent solution to my financial situation. So I started thinking.

I guess my "Eureka!" moment, such as it was, came one afternoon when I was watching the Oprah Winfrey show. That particular episode was a celebration of women who had become very successful by following their passions. I remember this had a huge impact on me after all, my only choice was to work for myself or get a job working for someone else, and the latter just wasn't an option as far as I was concerned.

"You're going to do what?" I can still remember Andrew's reaction the night I phoned him in England to tell him about my brilliant (I thought) idea of becoming a private investigator. Needless to say he didn't take me seriously; in fact no one did, especially the actual investigator I set up a meeting with to ask what I needed to do to get into the business. His advice was simple: "You are never going to make it because you are not an ex-cop; all private investigators in this country are ex-police. In fact the only kind of work you'd ever get would be relationship-related, infidelity stuff, and there's just not enough demand for that."

Whatever, I'd made up my mind. I had already lived a bigger life than any ex-policemen I knew; I could cope in any situation, I had an empathy with people, I was very intuitive, a good communicator – and more to the point, I just knew I could do it.

Arbeth & Co opened for business in 1996 as the first private investigation company in New Zealand run by a woman. My first staff members were all women too – my three daughters, Karoline, Annika and Louise – and my first job was investigating insurance fraud for one of the country's biggest insurance companies. Funnily enough, once the CEO had met me he didn't seem to mind that I wasn't an ex-cop. The job was a roaring success and others soon followed; the problem was my phone was also running hot with calls from people wanting me to do those relationship-related, infidelity stuff jobs that I'd been warned weren't out there. So I had to make a decision, and given where my strengths lay it was no contest: infidelity was going to become my specialty.

Andrew, meantime, was bombarding me with letters and phone calls: "I miss you and want to come out and see you." He was a man possessed or obsessed, I wasn't too sure. Well, to cut a long story short, Andrew came out to visit me and never left. Straight away he snared himself a highly paid professional job, moved into my cottage, and we were married in a local registry office in late 1996. But any happiness we had was very short-lived. Just weeks into our marriage, letters started arriving from his ex-wife: long letters and plenty of them. What was going on? The fact that he tried to hide them from me just made me more suspicious – after all, as you know, I've always believed that if you've got nothing to hide, you hide nothing. It didn't take me long to discover a bunch of those letters stashed away in his car: "It's wonderful you've found your El Dorado; just say the word and the boys and I will be out to join you." I couldn't believe what I was reading. Andrew's ex-wife and family were planning on joining him in New Zealand? What about me, his new wife? When I confronted Andrew his explanation was simple: "Don't pay any mind to her; she's just mad." But my intuition told me there was more to this than Andrew was letting on. We staggered along for a while, but four months later came the bombshell.

When Andrew walked into the house after a week away on a business trip, I knew immediately that something about him had changed; don't ask me how I knew, I just knew. I found receipts in his jacket pocket for all the meals he'd had while he was away. Nothing strange in that, you might say, but the problem was Andrew had told me he'd been so busy he had only eaten fast food all week and these receipts weren't from McDonald's, they were from top restaurants. What's more, they were for lavish meals for two people, meals that included quantities of cocktails. I felt sick to my stomach. Andrew had always been very affectionate to me, but now he was uninterested and preoccupied. So I started digging.

I began by phoning the restaurants in Christchurch where Andrew had eaten. Yes, they remembered him, a nice unmarried Englishman and his partner. Why, she was a local girl, and yes, they could give me her name. I rang the girl, and after I told her I was a private investigator she said that yes, she had met up with Andrew, but he'd told her he was divorced from his wife in England and had moved out to New Zealand to start a new life. He'd suggested that they keep in touch by letter, as he hadn't found himself a house yet. There was no mention of any wife in New Zealand.

Around this time, Andrew casually mentioned to me that his friend from Bristol, the one whose flat we had stayed at while she was away skiing in Switzerland, had married a doctor and moved to New Zealand – wasn't that a coincidence? So I got back on the phone, and it didn't take me long to track down Anne (not her real name). But what we shared in that phone call shocked us both. It emerged that at the same time as Andrew was living with me, he was also having a serious relationship with Anne. When Andrew had told me he was visiting his sons in Yorkshire every other weekend, he had actually been with Anne. And when he spent the weekends with me, he had told Anne he was in Yorkshire with his boys.

Anne was totally thrown by the fact that Andrew had taken me to stay in her house while she was away. "You only had to look in my wardrobe," she said, "and you would have seen all his clothes hanging there!" But that was just the start of what Anne had to tell me. She'd also been contacted by other women who'd had similar experiences with Andrew.

Andrew presented himself as a well-groomed, intelligent, articulate and empathetic man. But the reality was quite different: Andrew was a habitual liar who lived in a world of total secrecy. He was very narcissistic, and his only real interest, besides himself, was the pursuit of women. The problem was he could only fit in so many women each day, and if he wasn't already having an affair he was plotting his next one. Andrew had literally shagged his way around the world, creating havoc wherever he went. He'd had literally hundreds of affairs in dozens of countries; he actually didn't know how to be faithful, it just wasn't in his DNA.

I remember throwing my wedding ring out the car window into a paddock the day I confronted Andrew. Of course at first he denied everything, but in the end he realized I knew too much, and then he just sat with his head down like a sorry schoolboy. He never did offer me any explanation for his behavior; a mumbled "I don't know why I keep doing it" was the closest I ever got to an apology. Andrew moved out that day, but he didn't go far – just down the road in fact, and we kept in touch. Despite everything that had happened, I was the closest thing he had to a friend in the world.

The one aspect of my life that was going from strength to strength was my business. My husband might not have shown much interest in me, but the media sure weren't holding back. Just a year after our marriage bust-up, I was starring in a weekly reality TV show called you guessed it – Private Investigators, documenting my intriguing line of work. And if that wasn't enough, the girl who had left school at 14 signed her first book deal with a major international publisher. By the time 60 Minutes rang wanting my story, I felt like an old hand at this celebrity stuff.

But at the same time Andrew's life was falling apart even more, and a couple of years after our split he lost his job. I did some thinking; for all his many faults, Andrew was a very intelligent, capable and highly talented man. I remember that when I suggested he could do a little bit of work for me as a trial he could not believe I would even consider taking a chance on him, given our past. Of course my friends thought I had gone completely mad this time.

But what my friends and Andrew didn't realize was that I was a whole lot cleverer than they had all given me credit for.

I was sure I could turn Andrew's many personal faults into a positive gain for me and my business.

Andrew proved me right very quickly: he had a natural ability as an investigator. He might have wasted every other opportunity he'd ever had, but working for me he found his niche: if he had been good as a deceiver, he was even better at catching deceivers. Andrew knew every trick in the cheater's book, which didn't surprise me because he'd probably invented most of them. But over the years, as his part-time job with me turned into a full-time one, he turned out to be capable of any kind of investigative work. OK, I had to manage him closely, but curiously we worked together far better as employer and employee than we ever had as husband and wife, and in fact Andrew ended up being the best investigator I ever had.

One rainy morning in early winter 2009, I was driving into the city to meet up with Andrew and a client. He had been feeling under the weather for a couple of days, a touch of food poisoning, he thought. I rang him en route to see how he was: "I'm feeling a lot better actually; I'll see you in 20 minutes," he replied. Half an hour later my phone rang; it was a policeman. After he had confirmed my identity there was a pause, and then he said: "Julia, this is the call we hate to make, but Andrew is deceased." Andrew died of a massive heart attack on 13 May 2009, aged only 56. His remains were taken back to England, where he is now buried back in Yorkshire next to his father.

CHAPTER 11

How to spot a cheat at 1000 paces

This section of the book is a must-read for women young and old. These simple tips could save you from emotional and financial disaster, and untold stress. In other words they could actually lengthen your life because, as I noted earlier, living with high stress levels for a prolonged period can seriously reduce your life expectancy.

Actions speak the truth, not words

We've all heard the expression "Talk is cheap", but that's pretty hard to remember when someone you adore is whispering sweet nothings in your ear. However, in order to be protected from a con man – whether he's after your money or your heart – there is a great test you can do. If he's the kind of guy who talks a lot about what he's going to do, and in particular what he's going to do for you, treat him like a television set and put him on mute. Don't listen to what he says he'll do, but see what he actually does. An example of this is when someone you meet says they'll telephone you tomorrow. A week goes by and you hear nothing, then they call and say they have been so busy they haven't had time to call. Let's be honest, that's rubbish – it literally takes seconds to dial a number – but the number of people who use that excuse is huge.

Then you go out with someone and have sex together, but two weeks go by before you hear from him again. And when you do he comes up with all sorts of reasons why he hasn't been able to contact you. But let's be honest: the truth is that if you really want someone you'll contact them come hell or high water , just as if you broke your leg you would go to the hospital and have it fixed rather than hobble around for a day saying, "Oh hell , I haven't got the time."

Another example is when you're in a relationship with a guy and you've arranged to go out for dinner but he suddenly cancels, saying he thinks he's coming down with the flu. But, as chance would have it, one of your friends sees him at a restaurant with another woman. When you confront him his first response is to lie and say it wasn't him, but finally he admits he was there and gives you the story that he'd arranged to have dinner with his ex-girlfriend and felt you wouldn't understand if he told you the truth. It was easier for him to lie than tell you the truth. Again, the proof of his feelings is in his actions, not his words.

When someone shows you who they are, believe them

People will always show who they are in the beginning. It's just that often we don't see it, either because we're caught up in the excitement and emotion or we choose to ignore it. Instead we come up with excuses such as "Once we're married everything will be fine". But the paperwork doesn't change anything, because if there is a problem in the beginning of a relationship it's usually that problem that will end the relationship. Women in particular often spend their lives trying to fix things they have no control over. That's why, when you meet someone and you find in the beginning that they have a behavioral problem or a character flaw, you need to think long and hard about whether you want to pursue the relationship. If you choose to continue then you have to take responsibility for your actions.

For example, you meet the man of your dreams: he's single, has a good job, money in the bank, and loves kids, animals and you, so it seems. As your relationship progresses you discover he's not as single as you first thought, although he's quick to explain that the reason he told you he was single is that the relationship he is in has been over for ages. It's really a matter now of just moving out ... oh, and telling his partner of the last five years that their relationship has been in trouble for the last few months, as this will undoubtedly be news to her. So you figure he didn't want to hurt you by telling you the truth, and once he moves out and leaves her and moves in with you your problems will be solved. He tells you he loves you and thought he was doing the right thing, and that he'll never keep anything from you again. You accept his reasons and set up house with him. Three years on you start noticing little changes. He's not as attentive as he used to be. He gets quite aggressive and short-tempered with you, especially when you ask him where he's been or is going. You start to notice he can't go anywhere without his mobile phone and even takes it to the toilet with him. Once night you can't find him, but then you see him at the bottom of the garden standing in the dark talking on his mobile phone. Your mind flashes back to when you first met him and you remember how he would often call you late at night and you could hear road noise in the background. Eventually you find out he's been having an affair for the last year.

If you go back to the beginning of this story you'll see very clearly that he showed you who he was when he met you. He was already in a relationship and looking to set up another one. The question you should have asked yourself is, "If the relationship was so bad why hadn't he left already?" Because remember, "If they do it with you, they will do it to you." Humans are creatures of habit and this guy was just doing what he'd always done. That's why I say; the best barometer for the future is always the past.

There is no smoke without fire

If you hear a rumor about your new partner, especially from a family member or a friend, take heed because the saying is true: "There is no smoke without fire."

These are the cold hard facts you don't want to hear, especially when you have just met the most amazing person and everything seems so right. The last thing you need is me telling you that you've got it wrong, but the reason these people slip past your guard is that the moment your emotions come into play a large part of your common sense goes out the door. If you weren't touched on an emotional level you would not only see quite clearly what the problem is but you would be listening as well.

Wandering eyes

We all like to look at what we perceive to be an attractive person. That is a healthy and normal instinct. However, a problem arises when a man stares at someone else and his attention is taken away from the person he's with. Then, it becomes a warning sign.

I recently had a meeting with the husband of one of my clients, and it took me just 30 seconds to see that she had a problem. We met in a hotel foyer and before long I could have told you where every female was in that room. He couldn't seem to help himself. I found his behavior extremely rude, so imagine what it must feel like to be his partner and multiply that feeling tenfold. I don't even think he was aware of what he was doing;

he was talking to me but his eyes were all around the room. It's not much to expect that the person you are with gives you their full attention as a sign of respect. If your partner regularly shows signs of this behavior you have cause for concern. The same can be said of men who are forever commenting on other women in front of their partners. Again this shows a lack of respect, which goes hand in hand with infidelity.

Key points

- Take notice of what he does, not what he says he will do. A person's true intent lies in their actions, not their words.
- Don't ignore your intuition. If you have doubts about someone, take your time and get to know them before you act.
- Keep an open mind, listen and learn, and don't think you know someone when you have only just met them.
- Don't accept disrespectful behavior. There is a line between appreciation and showing disrespect to the person you're with.

Beware of the wolf in sheep's clothing

Cases like the ones I'm about to describe occur far too often for my liking. They always involve a vulnerable woman and a middle-aged man. The profile of the victim in these love crimes would be a woman who has lost her husband through either death or divorce, usually after many years of marriage. She will be financially secure, with freehold property and money in the bank, and will not have realized how terribly lonely she has become until the wolf enters her orbit. She will still have children around, but at this time in their lives they are very rarely living at home and may have families of their own. Once the wolf gets his foot inside the door he will use every opportunity to alienate the victim from her children and family. This is to stop any form of opposition to him, and she in turn will rarely listen to her offspring's protestation s, as she will feel they don't understand her need for male companionship.

There is a lesson to be learned here. In many of the cases we have investigated, the children have been on to the wolf long before the victim has, but they have felt powerless to do anything in the face of their mother's apparent, but misguided, happiness. However, in a number of cases it has been the family who has employed us to unmask the wolf.

The profile of the wolf is that despite all his years of working he has very little or nothing at all to show for it, bar money-making schemes, a high opinion of himself – and delusions of grandeur. He is what I would call a "would-be-if-he-could-be-but-never-will-be person".

He'll have a whole list of reasons why he's down on his luck, and in his mind it will always have been someone else's fault that the business venture went bust or he lost his home. He can be described as a financial opportunist, and often presents himself as either a charming rogue or a rough diamond – the exact opposite of the former husband or partner of his victim; I call it the "Lady Chatterley syndrome".

Some wolves don't have to do anything for their keep since many of their victims are so desperate for love and companionship they shower him with gifts and money. The wolf (who really has no feelings for them) treats them with disdain and contempt, yet still the gifts and money flow. The following cases are good examples of this behavior.

> **Margaret placed an advertisement in the local newspaper for a handyman, and with only one reply she allowed Frank to tidy up her small section and do some decorating around her apartment. She continued to find work for Frank, whom she always paid in cash, and this arrangement continued for some considerable time. They would always finish the day's work with a chat and a cup of tea, and during one of these conversations Frank told Margaret he didn't like apartment living. Margaret was beginning to have some feelings for Frank, who was the exact opposite of her late husband, a refined academic, and so she decided to move out of the apartment (which she really loved) and buy a house with some grounds. There were two reasons for this move – Frank didn't like apartment living and she was beginning to run out of things for him to do.**

Frank was in lodgings. He told Margaret he owned a home but was renting it out because it was way too large for one person to rattle around in. At this stage everything was platonic, but Margaret always made sure there was plenty of cold beer in the fridge and added a little extra to his pay to allow him a bet on the horses. But this was about to change.

Margaret was used to attending the theatre and wanted to take Frank out with her, but she was appalled by his clothing (his usual attire was black shorts and a singlet) so she bought him a whole wardrobe of clothes in a style she thought appropriate. Margaret never saw Frank wear the clothes, and later he told her he hated them and had given them to a charity shop.

Once Margaret had purchased the new house she had plenty of work for Frank, but the house was quite some distance from Frank's lodgings and he complained that his old car wasn't big enough to carry all his tools and materials. So Margaret bought him a bigger and better vehicle on the understanding that he would pay her $50 a week until the sum was repaid. By this time Frank knew he was on to a good thing and began to up the ante by asking Margaret for large sums of cash on the pretext that he needed new tools and equipment. Following each request Margaret would go to the bank and withdraw the money. She also paid for all their outings and gave him regular amounts of cash to spend on himself. All this was over and above the cash she paid him for work he did on the house and section.

Two things happened which should have soured the relationship. The first was when Margaret was taken seriously ill and called Frank to come over and take her to the hospital. Frank refused and was extremely abusive and cold. Margaret, in immense pain, managed to raise the alarm with some neighbors who called an ambulance. Frank refused to visit her, but this didn't dampen her feelings.

By now Frank was staying overnight at Margaret's place during the week, but she realized he never stayed over on Fridays and that he was unreachable at weekends. Although she visited his lodgings he was never anywhere to be seen. When she questioned him about this he replied, "You must be senile, woman; of course I was there."

He then began to criticize her constantly, and it appeared

that every thing about her annoyed him intensely. Yet Margaret was in love and overlooked his behavior, although not to the extent that she didn't ask for my help. This came about when he stopped all contact and refused to take her calls or visit her. Her request was to have him watched from Friday afternoon to see just where he went at the weekend.

On Saturday morning we followed him from his lodgings to a large house some 25 minutes away. He drove the car that had been purchased with Margaret's money into the driveway and picked up another woman of similar age to Margaret. Then he drove to a supermarket (where we noticed the shopping trolley was filled with beer and cigarettes), and we saw that at the checkout and later at the service station it was the woman who paid. Further checks revealed that the woman was the sole owner of the large house, and that she had been in Frank's life for five years and had left the property to him in her will.

When Margaret learned of the other woman she was devastated, but she still wanted Frank and told me she would have jumped out of a plane without a parachute if he'd asked her to, so deep were her feelings for him. In her mind this was a relationship, but unfortunately no one else would see it that way, least of all Frank, who simply saw her as an easy source of funds.

Not only had Margaret been funding his lifestyle with cash, but Frank was drawing a benefit and taking whatever his second victim offered as well. The tragedy of this story is that despite visiting lawyers (and spending more money) Margaret would take him back at the drop of a hat.

Valerie was a woman in her late fifties whose husband had been killed in a car accident, leaving her

a very wealthy woman by anybody's standard s. As a result of stress, she had become ill to the point of being unable to drive. Then along came Allan. He was the mechanic who had serviced her car, and he was interested in buying it when he found out she could no longer drive. When it came to paying for the vehicle, however, Allan couldn't afford the full amount, but he suggested that because Valerie couldn't drive he would offer his services to take her wherever she wanted to go as the balance of the payment. Valerie was prepared to accept this deal and so the arrangement began.

Again, Allan had a "rough diamond" kind of appeal, very different from Valerie's husband. The relationship became physical within a few weeks because Valerie had been starved of affection for a long time. This also allowed Allan to gain the financial maximum from the relationship in a very short time. He told Valerie he'd been living with his mother because his recent divorce had cleaned him out financially as his ex wife had got the lot and left the country. Valerie fell for his hard-luck story in a big way. Allan appeared to be all the things she had dreamed of and, true to his word; he drove her wherever she wanted to go.

After her husband's death, Valerie had been contemplating a holiday. When Allan played his sympathy card and complained of not being able to afford a holiday she jumped at the chance of time away with him and booked and paid for a trip away. In all they went away three times in the short period they were together, with Valerie paying every last cent. She later told me that in their time together he had never even bought her as much as a cup of coffee.

During their third trip away, Allan said he was keen to see an old school friend who lived about 500 miles to the north of where they were staying. Aware of Valerie's dislike of sitting in a vehicle for long period s, he said he would hire a car, go see his friend and be back in three days. Of course he didn't have any cash, so in addition to paying for the rental car Valerie gave him $1000. She was not to know that it wasn't an old school friend he was going to see but his ex-wife – with whom he'd been in constant contact and was on the verge of reconciling.

Part of Allan's plan was to get Valerie to buy him a house, and on their return he went into overkill in order to please her. But he was also becoming moody. He said it was because he was desperate to move away from his mother, but in truth it was because he only had weeks before his wife was due to return and he needed a house for her to move into. Allan was playing games with both of them, but Valerie was completely unaware of this and bought him a small cottage. He then asked if she would decorate and furnish the property. She duly obliged, using some of her own furniture which Allan had taken a shine to. However, it was at this point that she noticed he wasn't as available as he had been. When she asked why, he said the relationship was moving too fast for him and he needed space. This puzzled Valerie, especially as he had been so intense just a few weeks earlier.

Of course the reason Allan wasn't as available to Valerie was that his ex-wife had moved back and he had promised her they would be reconciled. This was the point where Valerie came to me and asked me to investigate.

Even now Valerie cannot accept the fact that Allan has done this to her. She believes the relationship between Allan and his ex-wife isn't physical, despite the fact that they are living together and have been seen out together.

There are similarities between Margaret and Valerie's stories in that neither woman can see that they played their part in allowing this to happen by buying affection. Both are going to play victim, saying quite vehemently that they will never trust anyone again. Therefore they could possibly spend the rest of their lives as very lonely women when there is no need. They should have done their homework first and exposed Frank and Allan for what they were – fraudsters.

When they get what they came for, these fraudsters suddenly cool off emotionally, become quite aggressive and can leave without a moment's notice, refusing to communicate in any way. This is their way of cutting dead the relationship, leaving their victim heartbroken. They then go on to squander their ill-gotten gains on projects that have a snowball's chance in hell of succeeding before beginning the search for their next victim.

Should you find yourself in this position, or if you are at the start of a relationship where you've noticed some of these warning signs, then do yourself a favor and don't accept at face value the hard-luck stories you're being fed. These men know how to play on a woman's sensibilities and vulnerabilities. You won't be the first, and if he has his way, you won't be the last. When we investigate these people we normally find a whole list of previous victims who have lost not only their hearts but also their homes and futures.

The number of clients who want me to sort out their financial woes long after the event are too many to count, and the vast majority have become victims because they have jettisoned their financial brain in favor of their emotional one.

When you enter into a relationship treat it as if you were starting a business, especially if you are independently in a strong financial position. Remember that when one company decides to take over another it doesn't do so without checking the financial standing and business systems of the company it intends to take over. It's called "due diligence", and if it's not carried out, "let the buyer beware".

When a financially independent woman meets what she considers to be the perfect man she should realize there is very little difference between entering into an emotional venture and a business venture, except that with the emotional venture comes the chance that both your emotional and financial well being are at stake.

Kate's story provides a lesson for any financially independent woman. We can all get wrapped up in the romance, the lust and the buzz of meeting someone new and not see the danger signs (and there are always signs). For Kate they were there right from the start, but she chose to ignore them.

At 54 and a widow, Kate had her own business and a string of properties. She was charming and self-assured with a great sense of humor, but she was also lonely and, as she pointed out, emotionally vulnerable. Friends had invited her to the local dance club many times and she had always refused, until one night she decided to placate

them by arriving unannounced – and that was the night she met Bill.

Bill was some ten years older than Kate but he was an excellent dancer and listened intently as, with the aid of a few glasses of wine, she told him all about herself – a big mistake. She then felt guilty that she had monopolized the conversation and began to ask him about his life, but she obtained little information from him except that he was a widower and a property developer. They agreed to see each other the following week and then began a relationship. Kate still knew very little about Bill; it was as though he had no history at all. Here was the first real clue that maybe there was more to Bill than met the eye.

They started to go away together at weekends, staying at a country lodge, and each time it would be Kate who paid for everything because Bill was always waiting for funds, which never materialized in time for him to pay his share. That was clue number two – such a thing might happen once, but more than that should have started the warning bells. Instead, Kate began to feel sorry for Bill, who was living in a partially finished house not far from her own, so she allowed him to move in with her despite the fact that she knew so little about him.

Soon they were working on a deal that involved selling most of her properties to fund an even bigger deal that would net them a large sum of money. The profit on this deal was huge, and at this stage Bill persuaded Kate not to place the funds in her own account but to open a joint account with individual signing rights so they could take advantage of further deals. This account was now flush with cash and wide open to abuse. This was clue number three, but again it was missed.

It was about this time that Kate's daughters decided to

voice their concerns to their mother. They argued that their collective gut instinct was that she was being set up for a financial fall. At this stage Bill had not contributed a cent towards housekeeping or the cost of outings, and he began to use the joint account without consultation, withdrawing hundreds of dollars a day.

When Bill got wind of Kate's daughters' disapproval he decided to move out and return to his half-built house, because the truth was that he was happy living there in semi-squalor and had never been happy living with Kate. He had done so only because he was after her money.

To Kate's knowledge Bill still had property developments of his own, which he had said were about to be completed. So even though he had left, she saw the time coming when they would pool their joint assets and live together. But then things began to change. Kate noticed that Bill had withdrawn a six-figure sum of money. When challenged, he said it was to complete his own house project, and that he would repay the money with interest when it was completed and sold. What Kate didn't know was that Bill was a bankrupt who had four ex-wives and owed creditors in excess of $250,000. The reason he had borrowed such a large sum from their account was not that he needed to finish the property, but to pay off creditors who were threatening to force a mortgagee sale if he didn't pay up.

By now most of the profits had gone from the account, and Bill was becoming less and less the charming rogue and more and more aggressive and distant. Kate admitted later that they had never actually consummated their relationship in the conventional way. But despite this he again managed to persuade her to fund a property investment, which would require all the remaining funds from the joint account plus remortgaging her freehold property. The warning bells were ringing so loud they would wake the dead, and Kate's daughters pleaded with her not to go ahead. But it was to no avail – Kate signed in good faith without reading the small print.

What Kate had signed was not what she had thought it was. According to Bill, the development had run into trouble and the money had been lost. Kate then found that Bill was unavailable when she called, and to this day she's never seen him again. She has lost virtually everything, and is fighting a long-drawn-out battle through the courts at even more expense.

Key points

Warning signs:

- A man in his fifties or older who enters your Life with a whole load of excuses as to why he has no assets.
- A man who asks for money, even if he says it's a loan.
- A man with no history [there is always history].
- A man who always seems to have no money at crucial moments.
- A man who is always waiting for the big pay-out, which never materializes.
- A man who suggests you invest in a business venture but doesn't feel it is necessary for you to know any details.
- A man you wouldn't normally be attracted to but for whom you make an exception because you're so lonely.

What not to do:

- Don't lose sight of who you are. Does this person have the same values, morals and ethics as you?
- Don't be indiscreet about your financial affairs.
- Don't try to buy affection.
- Don't think you can change who he is by changing what he wears.
- Don't dismiss as jealous gossip warnings to be careful because he's got a bad reputation.
- Don't ignore the concerns of your immediate family and close friends. Remember, they are Looking at the situation from an unemotional viewpoint.
- If you have a niggling, uneasy feeling even though you are very attracted to this person, listen to your intuition – it's rarely wrong.

Protection:

- Never sign anything without first taking it to your lawyer.
- Ask questions about him – get as much information as you can and check it out.
- If money or business ventures come into this relationship ask for his permission to do a credit check. If he refuses, that in itself is a warning. ["If you have nothing to hide you hide nothing."]

Financial betrayal

Betrayal comes in many forms. Emotional betrayal is bad

enough, but when it is combined with financial betrayal the situation can become too much, and it can lead to a breakdown in mental and physical health.

Lana, Raewyn and Lydia thought they knew their respective husbands well, but in actual fact not one of them had a clue about the emotional and financial blows their husbands were about to make them suffer until it was nearly too late. Each of these women became aware of the financial betrayal that was about to occur only when she attempted to discover if her husband was having an affair.

Lana's husband Barton was 63 and a prominent man in the city. Now approaching retirement, he had become involved at one of the city's largest educational establishments as a way of bridging the gap between his full-time business life and retirement some two years away. He and Lana had been married for more than 35 years, and their children were all married and living in various parts of the world. Lana knew Barton was struggling with the idea of retirement, so when he said he needed three months to clear his mind, and he wanted to visit Europe's art galleries and historical sites, she went along with his needs and supported him as she had done throughout their married life. Barton left for Europe, leaving Lana behind to run her own business.

The first warning signs arrived with his credit card statements. Although Lana knew Europe was expensive, she couldn't help but notice that the bills for meals were so high that no one person could have eaten so much. As the weeks went by the bills continued to roll in, and Lana told me of her concerns that Barton might just have someone with him. We discussed who this might be, and the only person she could think of was a visiting professor from Germany with whom Barton had spent an awful lot of time at a university function some six months earlier. He'd never mentioned this woman again, and hadn't given Lana any reasons to doubt him. However, after making a number of telephone calls to Europe we found that Barton did indeed have a travelling companion, and that her description, confirmed by staff at two of the hotels he had stayed at, matched the German professor.

Up to this point Lana was still convinced it was just a friendship, thinking that maybe they had joined up with each other for a few days to enjoy their mutual interest in Roman architecture. However, further investigations showed that they had met on Barton's first night in Europe and had been together ever since. Lana was deeply wounded by his deceit, and it took some days before she was able to come to terms with what had happened. When she did it was a different woman who approached the task of finding out exactly what was going on.

Barton was still only six weeks into his 12-week holiday and Lana wasn't about to let the next six weeks pass without finding answers to questions and concerns she had previously buried deep within. She began a systematic search of all their properties, offices, garages and lofts to see what she might uncover about her husband and the German professor. I was given a brief to search for all assets in his name and to continue to compile a dossier on his European trip for use later if the need arose.

It wasn't long before we had both made discoveries that rocked Lana to the very core. She had managed to hold up through the knowledge of her husband's emotional deceit, but the discoveries we made took her close to despair. During a search of his office, at the very rear of a small closet, Lana found a small cupboard. Inside was a document folder containing correspondence that showed Barton had been salting away funds and had set up a number of trusts into which properties and other valuables had been deposited. Legal documents showed he had been systematically planning a future without her for some eight years. My own investigations found that he owned two properties of which Lana had no knowledge – and to her horror both were owned jointly with the German professor.

However, the piece of paper that caused her the most anguish was a single A4 page in Barton's own handwriting where he compared the options of staying with Lana or starting a new life with his German professor. It was headed up "I've Been Thinking", and it concluded that Lana was worth very little despite their 35 years of marriage. One line in particular said: "What has she contributed to our wealth apart from being a mother to our children, tending the house and running a small business that makes a pittance? When we split, that cannot be worth more than 20 per cent of my wealth" – with the words "my wealth" underlined!

On his arrival back in New Zealand Barton didn't return home but set himself up in a motel, where he said he was taking further time out to decide on his future. Surveillance showed that in fact he spent no time at the motel whatsoever, but all his time with the German professor at one of their homes. The professor had in fact obtained residency some years earlier and had travelled on the same flight as him to Europe.

Raewyn and Heath, both in their late forties, had been married for 20 years and had two teenage sons. Heath ran a successful financial services company, while Raewyn was his support. She looked after their sons and helped entertain his many clients. To everyone, including Raewyn, Heath seemed the perfect husband and provider.

Then, during one of their many dinner parties for clients, Heath announced he had arranged a two-month surprise summer holiday trip for Raewyn and the boys to see her parents in the UK. Raewyn was delighted that Heath had gone to such lengths with the arrangements but wished he was going with them. Heath told her he'd recently taken on a number of new staff and, in his words, The business is expanding rapidly and it's very important that "I'm on hand to bed them in."

Raewyn was so busy preparing for the trip she missed vital signs that under normal circumstances her intuition would have picked up on. One week later she and her sons left for the UK.

Before leaving, Raewyn had agreed with Heath that she would con tact him every second day either at the office or at home depending on their itinerary. For the first week she managed to make contact as agreed. But on the second weekend one of the boys broke a bon e in his hand, so Raewyn telephoned home. There was no answer. Having tried the office with the same result, she rang Heath's mobile, which was switched off.

The following day she again tried all three phones with no luck. By this time she was becoming concerned and wondered if Heath had had an accident or had been taken ill. On the

Monday morning she telephoned his office, to be greeted by a new voice that seemed highly protective of her husband's whereabouts. When the young woman realized she was speaking with Heath's wife her voice became even more icy and protective. Finally, Raewyn was able to make contact with Heath, and asked where he had been during the weekend. His answer was that he'd been in and out, and the battery of his mobile had failed and he hadn't bothered getting a new one until that morning.

On two occasions during the following week Raewyn telephoned at night and on both occasions there was no answer. This was beginning to worry her, so she telephoned at 2 a.m. – again no answer. The following day she telephoned in the late evening and Heath was out, but he answered his mobile, saying he couldn't talk but would get back to her in a few minutes. When he did call back he was clearly out near a road as traffic could be heard driving by. His excuse was that he'd been in a business meeting and was now outside the hotel. By now Raewyn was beginning to have serious concerns about his whereabouts. It was the following day when the pieces of the jig saw puzzle began to fit into place.

Raewyn decided to telephone Heath's office and this time she was greeted by a friendly voice, not the icy tones that had greeted her last call. She asked the receptionist if Heath was available, only to be told he'd gone to lunch with Rochelle, his new assistant. Raewyn asked if it was Rochelle she had spoken to a few days earlier, and the receptionist said it would have been because Rochelle had been answering the phones while she had been away on a course. Raewyn then telephoned Heath's mobile but it was turned off. She finally telephoned home and there was no answer.

It was at this point that Raewyn telephoned me to ask if I could assist her. She began by telling me her story so far, and gave me her home address for surveillance purposes. It was then that I asked if she had a monitored alarm, to which she replied yes. My suggestion to her was simple: request a movement report from the alarm company, which would tell us at what times the alarm had been activated and de-activated. Within 24 hours I had a copy of the monitored alarm activations, and sure enough Heath hadn't been home when he said he had. In fact, the only time he'd been at home after Raewyn's first week away was the previous lunchtime when he'd been out with his new assistant. They had stayed for two hours. The report for that same night showed the alarm had not been activated.

We began surveillance outside Heath's office. On the first day we saw him emerge from the car park with a red-headed woman who looked about 20 years of age in the passenger seat beside him. But the vehicle did not match the description we had been given; instead it was a very expensive sports car. The car powered away, and eventually arrived at a luxurious new apartment complex with views over the ocean. Heath and his companion stayed the night there, and he drove the woman to the office the next morning. At lunchtime that day they drove to the family home, where once again they stayed for a couple of hours and then returned to the office.

We checked ownership of the apartment and the sports car and found that both belonged to Heath. We also carried out asset checks on Heath and completed a full business survey, which produced some extremely worrying results. We reported to Raewyn what we had found, but she was in denial and said we must be mistaken. We therefore asked her to arrange to speak with Heath at home each night for a week, so we could prove what he was up to. We stressed to her that she shouldn't give him any reason to be suspicious.

Each night that week Heath would drop his assistant at the apartment, drive home, answer Raewyn's phone call, then leave his home and return to the apartment where he would stay the night and then drive his assistant to the office the following morning.

At this point Raewyn left her sons in the care of her parents and returned home. Booking herself into a hotel, she arranged a meeting with me to try and come to terms with the emotional and financial situation we had uncovered. Before our meeting Raewyn hired a car and parked within viewing distance of her own home and sure enough, Heath and Rochelle drove up in the sports car, stayed for an hour and a half then left. When the coast was clear she entered her home and found the bed rumpled. She couldn't understand why he would bring someone back to the house when he already had a secret hideaway, unless it was for some perverse reason. She also found a remote control that she hadn't seen before. She immediately recognized it as a garage remote, and so together off we went to the beach house. As the door slowly opened it revealed a space filled with what could be called "big boys' toys", including two jet-skis, a pair of mountain bikes, water-skis, a small motor-boat and a whole pile of boxes filled with what were obviously Rochelle's personal belongings. Raewyn was stunned to see the expensive toys Heath had bought, because many of them were things he'd promised his sons but had always said they couldn't afford.

This was all the proof Raewyn needed. She visited a lawyer armed with our information, which showed Heath's business was in dire trouble and his spending was out of control. In fact, he was spending as if he had no financial problems at all. Raewyn then began the long journey many women have to travel when their husbands wreak financial and emotional havoc on their families.

We found that Heath had in fact met Rochelle two years earlier, and during that time she'd gone on overseas business trips with him during which he had spent lavishly on hotels, food, wine and gifts, including designer outfits and jewelery. He continued to maintain his excessive lifestyle until he filed for bankruptcy. He was asked to explain his extravagances and come to a settlement with Raewyn, but such was the tangled web of financial deceit that it took a forensic accountant to show just how he had deprived his family financially.

Throughout her married life Lydia had heard all the gossip about her husband Doug and various women with whom his work brought him into contact. Like many women who are the partners of influential businessmen, Lydia did her utmost to maintain her position in society and be seen as the dutiful wife who backed her husband to the hilt. She had all the trappings of her position and enjoyed these to the full. When the subject of her husband's infidelity came up from time to time she did her utmost to minimize, rationalize and justify his staying out later than he should, not being where he said he was, and the gifts and purchases on their credit card statements that never came her way.

So, when the rumors about Doug and his exotic-looking

secretary began, Lydia fell back into the role of dutiful wife and explained them as the words of people who were jealous of her husband's position at the very top of his industry. After all, she'd met the secretary at a number of functions and found her to be quiet and deferential. She didn't appear to be any threat to Lydia, despite being attractive and 30 years younger.

Unfortunately for Lydia, the persona portrayed by Aisha at the various functions was in stark contrast to the one that attracted Doug. Behind the deference lurked a smart woman who knew exactly what she wanted — and a powerful man like Doug could give her all those things. She'd known Doug was a player and found it easy to snare him.

While the rumors persisted, Lydia went about her life as though nothing was amiss. She wasn't overly concerned, as she and Doug shared joint ownership (or so she thought) of everything from their home and boat to rental properties, trusts and shares.

When Doug walked out on Lydia, he and Aisha had already set themselves up with a multi-million-dollar home overseas. Doug had also decided he no longer wanted to be based in his home country, and had moved his company's seat of power offshore. Lydia was totally unaware of what was going on. Doug was a master at hiding things and in the 18 months prior to leaving he had, with the help of his accountant, removed Lydia as the beneficiary of family trusts, changed the trustees and siphoned money into overseas bank accounts.

The catalyst for Lydia to call me was when Doug moved out of the matrimonial home and set himself up in an apartment, where he played the part of a recluse so well there appeared not to be any other woman in the picture. Despite Lydia's denial that anything was going on between her husband and his secretary, the old adage that there is no smoke without fire had us watching Aisha. Surveillance on her home was about to be called off when we saw her old car pull out of the driveway and set off in the direction of Doug's factory, where it then disappeared out of sight behind the main building. We waited for her to come out, but although a number of vehicles departed (the factory ran a late shift), including a silver Mercedes sport, Aisha's vehicle wasn't one of them. We called our colleague who was parked close to Doug's apartment and asked if he had anything to report. After initially giving a negative response, he then noticed that a distinctive Mercedes sport had just pulled into the underground car park – and guess what, it was the very same vehicle we'd seen at the factory.

At 5 a.m. the following morning the Mercedes, with Aisha at the wheel, drove from the apartment back to the factory, where Aisha picked up her own car and returned home.

The harsh cold facts of Doug's affair stunned Lydia, but she had only scratched the surface when it came to bad news. Lydia confessed she'd always let Doug handle the financial side of their relationship, although on closer scrutiny it appeared it was more a case of her having absolutely no say in what happened to their money. Doug had issued her with an allowance for housekeeping and personal expenses, but he handled all other expenditure. This had allowed him free rein, and he'd used it essentially to embezzle money from the marriage partnership. In addition to denying Lydia access to family trusts, her husband had made claims on property and valuables that were hers through a deceased estate. As well as facing a major battle to keep her head above water financially, there were emotional and personal issues for Lydia, plus a lengthy court battle to contend with in an attempt to sort out what was, under law, rightfully hers.

Because of the complexities of this case and Doug's ability to manipulate their financial circumstances to his benefit, Lydia found she was in no position financially or physically to keep the home that had been the cornerstone of their lives for more than 35 years. Devastated at losing the family home, she moved to a much smaller property. Now, having finally recovered from the double blow of losing her husband and her home, she is building her own life and exploring new possibilities — without, for once, the controlling figure of Doug.

It could be said that the clients whose cases are described above took their lifestyles for granted, and that they should have taken more care to ensure their financial futures were not compromised in any way. However, what is perfectly clear is that these women all played a full and equal part with their husbands in building the matrimonial estate, making it what it was at the time of separation.

In my view, while these women may have overlooked or missed important signs that suggested their husbands were betraying them emotionally, there were no signs that they were doing so financially. All three men went to great lengths to hide their betrayal, and carried out their deceptions over a considerable period of time. The length and depth of the deceptions had a specific purpose, which was to ensure their wives felt safe and content while they continued to undermine the trust these women believed was the foundation of their relationships. If it had not been for the seeds of doubt sown in relation to emotional uncertainty none of the three would have had any prior knowledge of the financial betrayal that befell them.

What is interesting in all three of these cases is that the men went to extraordinary lengths to hide their financial betrayal from their partners, and that this financial betrayal was the key to ensuring their futures with the new women in their lives. What should be of concern to all three mistresses was the degree to which each of the men deceived their wives. How would you feel as the mistress of one of these men, knowing that you, too, could be treated with exactly the same lack of feeling as the women who had given them unfailing support through the best years of their lives? Does a leopard change its spots? I think not. Therefore the new women in their lives must surely be concerned as to how long they will last and how secure their financial futures will be. I would advise each one of them to take great care to ensure they have financial independence, because as they age and the novelty wears off they may become less attractive to their men, and the chances are that "Having done it with them, they will do it to them". And if that saying isn't sufficient try this one on for size — "The best barometer for the future is the past".

How do you protect yourself against financial betrayal?

- Consult a family law specialist and set out exactly what you consider to be the assets of the marriage. Prepare the documentation thoroughly so you don't waste time and money.
- Make sure joint signatures are required on check accounts.
- Have all bank statements sent to your home address.

- Have all credit card statements sent to your home address.
- Know who both your bank manager and your accountant are.
- Regularly have independent checks made on any trusts, especially when you and your children are beneficiaries.
- Ensure that mortgages are as they should be. We regularly see clients who find their husband has taken out loans against the family home or has remortgaged the home to fund other ventures.
- If you have any suspicions, have someone check your husband's assets register – especially for property.
- You should consider having a caveat on any property you consider a risk.
- Take note of any shares or bonds you hold, and check regularly to make sure they haven't been sold without your knowledge.

Internet infidelity

If there's one factor that's changed the face of infidelity in the last 15 years, it's the internet. It used to take a long time to meet partners and for relationships to form; nowadays the internet allows anybody to find dozens, even hundreds of potential partners with the click of a mouse. Infidelity doesn't always have to be physical to be betrayal; it just has to be something that removes you from your relationship.

Internet relationships often become very intimate very quickly because inhibitions are lowered – people on the net aren't face to face with each other, so the visual cues that are normally such an important part of meeting someone new don't apply. Often by the time people do meet in person they have formed strong opinions or expectations that may override their normal reaction to the kind of person they are meeting.

> **"Hi, I'm Mark; I am 56, single, athletic and good-looking. I am six feet tall and have a full head of my (own!) hair. I work for a respected company in a position of trust and I am required to travel all over the world for business. I live in a small community close to the sea and enjoy cooking, music, good wine and companionship. I am seeking someone from 35 to 55 for a committed relationship."**

When Jan read Mark's profile on a dating site he sounded ideal. When she saw his photograph she was quietly surprised – his looks matched the description he'd given exactly. She contacted Mark and they quickly struck up a rapport via email. They seemed to have such a connection. Jan was thrilled when things developed very quickly. Before she knew it she was in the throes of a full-on sexual love affair. Mark was a passionate and skilled lover who certainly knew his way around a female body. He was just amazing!

So how do I know about all this? Well, a few months after the relationship started, Jan contacted me for some advice: there was something that was starting to really bother her. Despite the fact that she and Mark had declared their love for each other after only a couple of months, Jan had still not seen Mark's house. She had his mobile phone number, but not his home number. In addition, Mark had told her he was working on an international job that required him to be up all night on the phone, so he couldn't see her as often as he'd like. What should she do, she asked me.

I suggested we do a bit of overdue due diligence on Mark. We checked out Jan's new lover, and — surprise, surprise — things weren't what they seemed. Mark lived by the sea all right, but not in his house. He was actually renting a room at his ex-wife's place because he didn't have two cents to his name. All his money had been spent on the pursuit of sexual gratification: wine, women and clothes. Yes, he did travel occasionally for work, but not as much as he'd claimed on his profile. In fact, it seemed the real reason he'd mentioned he was away on business a lot was to provide him with a cover to pursue other love interests on the net. It turned out] Jan was one of nine women Mark was in love with.

How well do dating sites screen their customers to make sure they are who they say they are? There are some rules and regulations out there, but you'd have to say not many, especially after you've read Michelle's story.

Michelle and Gary had been married for 20 years. They had a beautiful home, three lovely kids, and as far as Michelle knew, they were happy.

Michelle never used the computer in Gary's home office, but one particular day she needed to. When she logged on, an email notification popped up saying there was a new message. Without thinking, Michelle clicked to open it. She found herself reading a message a strange woman had sent to her husband — an invitation to meet. As you can imagine, that got Michelle fired up so she went through the computer's usage history to check on just what her loving husband had been up to online. What she discovered was all bad: screeds of email correspondence between her husband and other women. That's when we were called in.

Because the computer was matrimonial property, i.e. it belonged to both Gary and Michelle; we suggested she have it forensically examined to give her a full picture of what was going on. The subsequent report from my computer forensic expert was inches thick. His research showed Gary had been online trawling for casual sex on average four hours a day for many years. There were emails and photographs from over 6000 women with whom Gary had been in contact. We also found travel bookings and hotel receipts that corresponded with Gary's online activities. Gary had been deceiving Michelle and his family for a long time.

So what about the people who ran the dating site – did they know or care that Gary was married? Well funnily enough our computer forensics told us they did. The site administrators knew Gary was married because his profile said so. It was the only honest thing Gary had done in the whole exercise; but he had described himself as married only because he was looking for casual sex, no strings attached. That had drawn an angry response from other customers on the site who were singles looking for real romance; they had demanded the site's owners remove Gary's profile. So you know what Gary did? He just changed his online status from "married" to "single" and the site administrators, the customers and of course Gary were all happy.

But Michelle wasn't happy – far from it. Despite all the evidence presented to him, Gary denied everything. He'd had a look on one of those sites once or twice, he said, but he hadn't actually "done" anything. As far as Michelle was concerned, however, Gary had done enough to end their marriage.

But there are actually sites out there that cater

specifically for married people who want to cheat without their spouse ever knowing anything about it. One successful site is run by a man who describes himself in his bio as happily married; he doesn't see any moral dilemma in the fact that his business is based on marital deceit.

The simple fact is, the growth of the internet means more people are spending more time online chasing more and more opportunities to interact. Like on the role-playing sites, the artificial worlds like Second Life where people can go online and create fantasy lives for themselves as other people. Second Life is just what it says – a virtual second life that a lot of people seem to prefer to the real thing. How sad is that?

In a recent television documentary an American woman admitted to spending up to 14 hours a day immersed in Second Life; unbelievably, she was married with teenage kids. Her husband worked and ran the household; the kids could only communicate with Mum if they hung out in her bedroom where the computer was. On Second Life this overweight middle-aged housewife had transformed herself into a slim space nymphet who was involved sexually with another user who was online as a god-like warrior. He was actually an unemployed working class 30-year-old from England. Because this couple were so immersed in their characters they were naive enough to think their relationship could work in real life. Unfortunately when they did meet the fantasy was well and truly shattered.

It all just goes to show the level of deception – and self-deception that the internet can encourage. But the technology is not to blame; it's the way it's abused by individuals.

Brides are us?

There is no doubt many happy relationships that are formed from so called "mail-order bride" sites on the internet. Chinese, Japanese, Thai, Russian, English, Czech – you name it, there's a mail-order bride site for every nationality under the sun. But for every pairing that works, I see a dozen that don't. Why do so many men have such unrealistic expectations when it comes to what they are looking for? These sites are often honey traps for middle-aged men of modest means who believe that attractive 20-plus-year-old foreign girls are desperate to form love relationships with them. Why would such girls really want to get involved with older men from halfway round the world? The answer is often depressingly simple, of course: money.

There are a couple of key warning signs for men who may be tempted by what they see on offer on the bride sites. They may sound blindingly obvious, but you would not believe how many men ignore them. If a girl you are interested in posts photos of herself in semi-dressed or undressed poses, it's a clear sign of what her agenda is. And secondly, direct requests for money, no matter how tragic the circumstances, should always sound an alert.

Key points

- The internet is a haven for emotional cheats.
- Profiles in dating sites are Like CVs! Check them out thoroughly.
- If you are going to physically meet someone you have met

on the internet make sure you do it in a very public place and tell a friend where you are going.

Financial love cheats on the net

I've already warned you about the emotional love cheat who is out to steal your heart, or, if caught, to break his wife or partner's, but there's another type of cheat out there. These people inhabit the same chat rooms and dating sites, but they're not really interested in you for your looks and sexual preferences (although that's where they'll start) – they're interested in your money, property, and in fact any realizable assets you have. I've talked about this kind of person and what to watch out for in the section "Beware of the wolf in sheep's clothing", but on the internet it's more difficult. You may be dealing only with words. And even pictures can be of someone else and not the person to whom you think you're talking.

This form of cheat will be looking for women or men of independent financial means, and it's amazing how much information they can gain prior to any meeting. The reason for this is simple; the internet is so informal that people tend to open up far more freely than they might in more formal surroundings. Sending photographs of your house or discussing the type of business you own gives the net predator the opportunity to decide if there are pickings to be had. Watch out for the man or woman who, after a reasonable period of time during which you have formed an internet relationship, gives you a small hard-luck story which requires you to send them something like $100, just to get them through the next few days. They will generally repay this money immediately, but that's just part of the test to see if you will go along with their scam. If you don't, you'll find their interest in you will cool very quickly. If you do, you'll find their needs continue.

Despite years of wrenching and lurid coverage in the media, and the numerous sites online which publish the photographs and personal details of known internet love scammers, thousands of supposedly sensible men and women around the world fall for bogus online romance every year. Nearly every week it seems there is another news headline reporting that an "Elena from Kirov" or a "Supanee from Bangkok" has vanished with their new spouse's life savings after a whirlwind online romance, leaving devastation in their wake. I have to say that men are quite simply suckers for this type of scam as their little head rules their big head and their need to be attractive to women makes them easy prey.

If you do end up meeting your internet friend then protect not only your financial assets but also your emotional ones, because when someone is after you for financial gain they'll try emotional deception first. If in doubt, refer back to the section "Beware of the wolf in sheep's clothing" and use the checklists to detect the cheats from the good guys or girls.

Key points

- Never give out personal financial details over the net.
- Be careful how much personal information you release.
- Never send money to someone with a hard-Luck story.
- If it sounds too good to be true, it generally is not true.

Predators on the net

Generally, when people talk about betrayal they assume it takes place between two adults. However, with the internet it is dangerous to assume anything.

My clients' 16-year-old daughter was spending every waking hour on the net. It all started quite innocently on her part when she entered a chat room and began to chat with someone who, judging from his profile, was of a similar age.

They quickly struck up a friendship, and little by little snippets of information came through suggesting he was a few years older than she was (25 years older to be precise). But by this time she didn't care how old he was as they were firm friends. Then the mood of the conversations changed and he admitted to having strong feelings for her. He said this had never happened to him before, and she was a very special person to arouse these feelings in him. (Ideal with adults who fall for this crap, so is it any wonder that an impressionable 16-year-old girl was head over heels in love by this stage?)

The relationship moved from friendship to sexual – which had been his intention from the start. She was now saying and doing things a 16-year-old would not normally know about without a coach. It was at this point that her parents noticed a change in their once fun-loving and carefree daughter. She had become reclusive and had isolated herself from her usual group of friends at school. She found it impossible to relate to anyone, and couldn't reveal her secret and sordid life with her older lover. Her schoolwork was suffering badly as she now spent most evenings and into the early hours talking on her mobile phone or sending text messages to him.

This man was an evil predator who had spun his magic and she was totally besotted with him. He began to up the sexual ante and had her purchase a web camera so he could watch her perform depraved acts. All this was being done without her ever having seen a picture of the man she was performing for, such is the power of these sexual predators.

It was no surprise to us to find this man was married with children and another on the way. He hadn't held down a job in years and it was his pregnant wife who was the breadwinner. They were in serious financial trouble, and her parents had had to bail them out more often than they could afford.

When we spoke to his wife she told us he had a history of infidelity both on and off the internet, and that he had betrayed his first wife with her ("If they do it with you they will do it to you"). The information we were able to give her actually came as a relief, as she had known for years that their marriage was in serious trouble and with the support of her family this was enough to give her the strength to leave him.

Our clients were able to persuade their daughter into therapy, but the road will be a long one for her. Unfortunately when we went back into the net there he was, larger than life, working his magic on his next victim.

Key points

- Keep a close watch on your children and make sure that you have free access to the computer area when teenagers [especially girls] are on the net.
- Teenage girls are easy prey for predators.

Internet detectives

The internet, computers and mobile phones may have made it a lot easier for people to cheat, but they've also given people like me and my operatives a lot of new ways to catch them.

The technologies that are now available to cheaters are fantastic — take so-called Tiger Texting, for instance. This is mobile phone software that automatically deletes texts as soon as you send or receive them. Download it off the net straight onto your mobile — if your suspicious partner examines your phone there'll be no evidence you've ever sent or received anything dodgy.

Great news for cheaters, you'd think, but as always there's a catch. You see the technology may be great, but it's still being used by a fallible human being who will exhibit the same old behavior — checking their phone constantly, never letting it out of their sight or turning it off when you are around, walking out of earshot when a call is received, or simply never bringing their mobile into the house. Many unfaithful partners also have two mobile phones, one for work and another for pleasure.

So just how private is a mobile phone? How easy is it really to recover data from a cell phone? I asked one of my specialized technicians — an expert in data recovery — to give you an insight.

A very common request nowadays is to undertake an examination of a mobile phone. This is not surprising considering the quantity and type of data that can be stored on a modern handset.

My biggest problem with mobile phone examinations is the client's expectations. While television programs like CSI give an insight into what can be achieved in forensics, they can also give people unrealistic expectations.

Mobile phone data can be stored in three different places. There is the handset memory, the SIM card, and the removable memory card. Most of the data like text messages is stored on the handset itself. The memory chip for storage of this data is limited in capacity, and deleted data is quickly overwritten with new data. The odds on recovering a deleted text message from three months ago are very small.

The amount of data that can be stored on a SIM card is increasing all the time, and deleted text messages that had been stored on a SIM card are more easily recoverable using forensic tools. Unfortunately, few mobile phone handsets actually store this data on a SIM card.

The removable media cards found in more advanced mobile phone handsets have a file system similar to that of a computer. This means that traditional computer forensic techniques can recover the deleted information from these cards.

As with any computer forensic examination, there are no guarantees about what data will be recovered. I've conducted an examination where the client requested details of deleted text messages. When the phone was examined I was unable to recover this detail; however, I was able to recover deleted video from the removable media card. This video more than confirmed that the client's partner was having an affair!

There are plenty of other pieces of information relating to mobile phones that do not require a forensic examination. Scrutinizing the mobile phone bill can show all sorts of pointers about your partner's behavior.

After we suggested that one client review the mobile phone accounts, he returned to tell us that he had checked the accounts over the last 12 months. Eight months ago the average number of text messages being sent each month was 300, a figure which then rose suddenly to nearly a thousand messages a month. Another client commented that her partner received lots of text messages, but when she accessed the hand set all messages had been deleted.

Call logs are another source of intelligence. While many handsets require the occasional deletion of text messages to free up memory space, this is not the case for the call logs. If you are regularly checking the call logs on a handset and they are not displaying a list of received calls and dialed numbers, then you should be suspicious.

You would also expect that a phone's contacts, or phonebook as it is sometimes known, would contain names associated with regularly dialed numbers. Don't be fooled by a male name being associated with a number that you suspect is that of your husband's girlfriend. Many times this simple deception has convinced a suspicious partner that there is nothing to worry about.

When you find emotional infidelity, nine times out of ten you find financial infidelity. But say you're in a relationship or marriage where your partner, not you, handles the money side of things. Even

if you can check your bank accounts, that still doesn't mean you know everything that's going on. You may have no idea just what your partner's, or your, true financial status is. You may have more assets than you realize – or you may have more debt!

That's why having the family computer forensically examined is one way to help you put the pieces together. Again, my expert takes up the story:

> *Probably the most common computer forensic examination I undertake in relation to a marital situation is to follow the money. It would be unusual for one party in a marriage to up and leave without some form of pre-planning.*
>
> *The time between one party deciding they will leave the marriage and actually doing so could be many years. During this time, I have often found that they will have considered the financial implications of a 50-50 split, and not liked the outcome.*
>
> *They may well open additional bank accounts, invest in shares, or even purchase property without their partner's knowledge. A forensic examination of the computer system may identify details of this type of behavior.*
>
> *On one occasion I received a request from the ex-wife of a failed finance company director. Her ex-husband was claiming to be bankrupt, and saying there were no assets to divide. She did have the family computer system, however, and she asked me to examine it for details of any assets.*

One of the processes that I conduct is to examine all the files on a computer system to identify if any are encrypted. This is called an entropy test. After running an entropy test and identifying 12 encrypted files, the next task was to break the encryption and view the content of the documents.

Setting up special software that will conduct a brute force attack on the password of the encrypted document, I left the password-cracking software running over the weekend – this software was trying different passwords at over one million per second. I was able to decrypt each of the encrypted documents, revealing details of offshore bank accounts not previously known to the ex-wife.

Identifying encrypted documents is just one method of following the money. While each job is different, many of the stories I hear and the requests I receive are the same. Money and assets are being hidden to avoid their having to be shared with the ex partner.

One recent case I examined involved a couple who had been married for over 20 years. They were financially sound, with the family home being worth many millions of dollars. The husband had recently advised that he was leaving the marriage and was looking for a new place to live. Again, I was asked to check the family computer system to establish details of any assets that were not known to the wife.

By examining files that had been deleted from the computer, I was able to establish that the husband had been planning his exit from the relationship for over five years. He had bank accounts and a property salted away. The purpose of hiding these assets was to avoid having to split them with his wife upon separation.

There are many reasons people become suspicious of what their partner may be doing on the internet: you may notice a porn site ad that pops up out of nowhere when you log in, or perhaps a dating site among your emails. Maybe your partner just seems to spend an awful lot of time on the computer late at night. Child pornography, internet predators, adult chat rooms, online dating sites – if it's on the internet it could be on your computer. Having your computer examined by an expert can not only provide proof of such activity, it can also give you peace of mind when it counts.

Rochelle and Dave entered my office together carrying a laptop computer. Rochelle's eyes were red and I could tell neither of them had had much sleep in a while. Dave said up front that he would let Rochelle explain their situation, but he couldn't help interrupting and leading the discussion. However, Rochelle did manage to explain that a little over a year earlier Dave had had an affair, but this had ended when she discovered what he had been up to. Although she believed that he was now faithful and she trusted him, she had recently found information in his web-based email account that concerned her.

At this point Dave chimed in and said that the email

account in question was one that he had used to communicate with the woman he had the affair with, but he had not used this account since breaking up with her. Although Rochelle said that she now trusted her husband, she had been investigating his computer to ensure he wasn't seeing someone new.

Dave was insistent that he had not used this email account in over a year, and in an effort to put Rochelle's mind at ease they had come to me to have the computer forensically examined. My immediate thought was that Dave must not understand the capabilities of our computer forensic examiners – he must be naive if he believed we would not find evidence of what he had been up to.

While most people understand that a computer forensic expert can see the content of files that have been deleted, they do not always realize that this extends to recovering details of their deleted email messages and a chronological list of the websites that have been visited.

I always report my findings once the forensic examination has been done, and I don't prejudge the outcome. However, in this case I was surprised to find that the only access to Dave's alternative email account was in the last couple of days, when Rochelle had accessed it using one of Dave's common passwords. The last access prior to this was over 12 months earlier, just after Dave had called off his affair.

Further examination revealed that within a couple of days of the affair ending Dave's web-based email account had been accessed from a different computer by someone other than him, and there were a number of email subscriptions associated with his email address. These subscriptions were for transsexual newsletters, which had been arriving in his email account on a regular basis ever since. Because I could prove Dave himself had not used the account since ending his affair 12 months earlier, I knew he had no idea that this had been happening. I was able to assure Rochelle that Dave had had no inappropriate access to websites or email communication in the last 12 months.

This case was unusual because both partners made their request for a forensic examination together. It was also unusual because the evidence was in support of the person under suspicion. As with any computer forensic examination, you never know what you are going to find until you look – this was a good example of someone with a little computer knowledge – in this case Rochelle – conducting their own investigation and coming to the wrong conclusions.

> **Another useful tool in the modern PI's arsenal is the GPS. GPS stands for Global Positioning System, and the tracker is a small device that can be attached to a car or boat, which emits an electronic signal which enables the whereabouts of the vehicle to be monitored. The GPS tracker even sends the exact address of where it is at any time, right down to the street name and number. It definitely makes a PI's job easier, though different countries have different privacy laws and they all have to be taken into account before a GPS unit can be used. There are a couple of other snags: getting the GPS unit on and off without being spotted can be a problem, and the significance of the addresses where the vehicle goes still needs to be confirmed.**

And that's the thing about all this technology – it's fantastic, but the one thing it can't replace is the human element. While a GPS tracker, for example, can tell you where a person is at any given time, it can't tell you what they're doing there and whom they are with. It takes a good old-fashioned human being to tell you that.

CHAPTER 12

How to have an affair

While I was writing this book I mentioned to a man that I was including a chapter on how to have an affair, and he immediately commented that men wouldn't need to read this chapter because they were the ones already having affairs. I replied: "No, you don't get it. They might be doing it, but they need to read this chapter more than women because they are the ones who are getting caught." It took a few seconds but then I saw the penny drop.

So in this chapter I am going to endeavor to give you some guidelines on how to have an affair that will perhaps keep you from being caught. Whichever way you look at it there are some fundamental rules that have to be followed in order to successfully carry off an affair.

Let me explain why I'm devoting time to this subject and reassure you that it's not as bad as you may think. When it comes to deceit, human nature is the cause of most people's downfall. If we were all emotionless creatures, firstly there would be no need to concern ourselves with relationships, and secondly we could all be successful betrayers. In order to deceive, there are some very basic rules that must be followed religiously and even then they're not foolproof because there are other factors that come into play. One only has to look at the things people do that get them caught or exposed and work backwards from there — but that's a whole lot harder than it sounds. Remember what I said in my introduction: the perfect affair, like the perfect crime, does not exist.

I guess it's like someone living in poverty for most of their lives and then suddenly winning a lottery. It would be almost impossible for them not to do something that would alert people to the change in their circumstances, no matter how hard they may try. Any change, whether subtle or obvious, is what will first alert someone to the reality of a new situation. Therefore, if you're going to have an affair it is crucial to act exactly as you did the day before meeting Mr. or Ms Wonderful.

The rules

Rule 1 - Honesty

Honesty is an essential ingredient in conducting a successful affair. Know it sounds ridiculous talking about honesty in the same breath as deception but it is necessary.

How many times do married men pose as single men to attract women (usually single women)? This behavior is, quite simply, courting disaster. Single women are looking for a relationship and commitment, whereas married men are acting indulgently and look for self-gratification and nothing more. If you're married and posing as a single man it won't be too long before you blow your own cover because your lover is going to start asking questions. These questions will take one or more of the following forms:

"Why won't you stay the night?"

"Why can't we see each other at the weekend?"

"Why don't you give me your landline number instead of just your mobile?"

"Why can't we go back to your house?"

"Where is your house?"

I don't need to tell you what's going to happen to you when your lover finds out she's been lied to – I'll leave that to your wife.

Rule 2-Don't enter into any sort of a liaison, from a one-night stand to a long-drawn-out affair, with anyone in your workplace

Affairs are only that – they don't last and they aren't meant to last. Remember, only five per cent of men leave their wives for a lover, and when they do these relationships rarely last. Do you really want to end up having to face that person on a daily basis after an affair has turned sour? And is the potential risk to your other life really worth it? No office affair ever goes unnoticed by colleagues; therefore the chances of a disgruntled workmate spilling the beans to your partner are high.

This rule also applies to your social circle, which may appear on the surface to offer the perfect opportunity to conduct an affair with someone who's already known to you and where the odd casual sighting may be easy to gloss over. This isn't the case, however, and it's virtually impossible to carry off since friends who see you on a regular basis will notice even the subtlest of signs. Playing too close to home is a recipe for disaster.

Rule 3-Never get lost in the haze

You need to be very clear about what you want from your affair and what you want from your marriage. Never under any circumstances should they merge. Your home life is exactly that — your life where you live with your wife and family. It is secure and comfortable, the practical stuff of day-to-day living. Your affair, on the other hand, is based on passion, sex and excitement. These are two very different worlds; therefore their identities must remain separate.

Don't fall into the trap of talking about how hard it is at home when in fact it isn't. I find men do this all too often when generally it's simply a throwaway line. Women take words so literally that going down this path is sure to backfire. Never discuss your home life with your lover, just as you would never discuss your lover with your wife. It will only come back to haunt you.

Rule 4-Don't buy yourself into a hole

I find most men can't help themselves; they just have to buy something special for the new woman in their life no matter how temporary she may be. It's an ego thing, and a sure-fire way to fall flat on your face.

There are two reasons for this. Firstly, the effect on your lover is that she is going to wish she could meet someone as wonderful and generous as you with whom she could fall in love permanently. Secondly, she'll have ongoing expectations even if you started off the right way by stating the ground rules first.

Action such as giving her presents will send all that good work out the window. She'll start reading far more into it than you realize or ever intended. Your wife, on the other hand, will find out — as they inevitably do.

I'm surprised at how many men pay for gifts for their lovers with their credit card. I've lost count of the number of times a wife has found receipts for jewelery and, in typical female style, has nearly always given her husband the benefit of the doubt, thinking it must be a late birthday or anniversary present, or just an "I love you" present. Alas, it never comes home.

I recall one client who knew her husband was having an affair. However, when she found the credit card statement from his recent overseas business trip she noticed he'd purchased an extremely expensive Burberry woman's coat. Understandably she became rather excited because she couldn't imagine he would spend that kind of money on his floozy. As time went by and the coat never materialized she knew she was wrong. But, again in true female style, she lived in hope until one day in her husband's office she noticed a picture on his PA's desk. It was a photo of the PA wearing — you've guessed it — the very latest Burberry coat.

Rule 5-Don't foul in your own nest

It astounds me how many affairs are carried out in the matrimonial home. I've heard a million times from my clients, "My husband would never bring anyone back here." Well, I'm sorry to be the bearer of bad news but the facts are the facts and I see it time and time again.

If you're going to foul in your own nest and you don't want to be discovered then you have to be very vigilant. If you put some of your wife's possessions away before your lover arrives then make sure you put them back exactly where you found them, and make sure you clean up after yourself — but not to the extent Carol's husband did. She'd been away for a week with the kids visiting family over the holidays while her husband Ted stayed in the city because of work. When Carol got back the house was spotless, and she was very impressed that he'd made such an effort. It was two or three days before she noticed a strange G-string in her underwear drawer. It was strange since it wasn't at all Carol's taste in underwear, and it wasn't even her size. She agonized over how it could have got there, and by the time she rang me she'd conjured up every scenario imaginable.

It was later discovered that while Carol and the kids were away Ted was entertaining an escort in the house and the G-string belonged to her. It clearly showed how little this husband knew about his wife's taste in underwear – if he'd taken more notice it would have cost him less grief.

Not only is stray underwear a problem – earrings, bracelets, lipsticks and other personal items left by your lover inadvertently or by design can catch you out. Make sure that if you find anything that doesn't belong to your wife you dispose of it away from the house. Check inside pillowcase s, the medicine cabinet, bedside drawers and bathroom vanity areas and behind and under the bed.

Many an affair has also been foiled by a nosy neighbor behind lace curtains, because Neighborhood Watch is alive and well in the suburbs.

Rule 6-Beware the little things that make each of us unique

I mentioned earlier that other factors come into play when trying to keep an affair undetected. No matter how hard you try to do everything in your power to act as though nothing has changed and you are just the same today as you were yesterday, there are some things that are simply out of your control. So beware – your body can betray you, as Susan explains:

> *I was fortunate, on reflection, in that I had already suffered two previous affairs so my intuitive antennae were already primed when the signals started falling into place. The final straw and actual confirmation that he was playing around was the most obvious one – sex! We had become in a lot of ways more like brother and sister and our sex life had become something I instigated as a form of love and affection. If he hadn't had sex for a couple of weeks he had a habit of farting when he ejaculated, but if we had sex frequently this didn't occur. All of a sudden I noticed his farting had ceased no matter how long the intervals between us having sex. That's when I knew for certain.*

So, essentially, even if Susan hadn't had the previous betrayals to heighten her awareness that John was playing around, his body would one day have given him up to his fate. You may not be aware of your idiosyncrasies, but your partner will be.

Rule 7 - There's no such thing as a secret when two people know

I'm sure you've all heard the saying "Loose lips sink ships". In other words, the only people who need to know about your affair are the two of you.

Men are prone to letting their egos get in the way, and often when under the influence of alcohol they'll brag to their mates about their most recent conquest. Women have a permanent grin and that faraway look in their eyes when they meet friends for coffee, which leads to questions they don't want to answer but often do.

Human nature is a curious thing and jealousy is a destructive emotion. Although they may be your friends, your happiness can create more problems than you bargained for. It only takes a few words for problems to occur and your ship to go down, so resist the temptation to share your affair with anyone.

Rule 8-Don't leave a paper trail

The computer can be your worst enemy, so ensure you don't communicate with your lover via your home computer. Even if you think you've deleted all the email evidence, a forensic computer expert will be able to retrieve it without any problems whatsoever.

Don't password the home computer. One of the most important rules is: "If you have nothing to hide you hide nothing." The most obvious indication that you have something to hide is a password on the home computer that only you know.

And don't think that just because you bin your mobile phone bills you're in the clear. If you're asked to prove your trustworthiness by allowing your wife to view your phone records, saying you can't find them won't cut the mustard. Records are kept for seven years, and a simple phone call to your telephone company will reveal all.

Rule 9-Choose your lover carefully

The next fundamental strategy is your choice of lover, and that choice is critical to the success or failure of an impending affair – so choose your lover wisely. This is another potential area for disaster, so make sure the person you choose is emotionally mature, emotionally stable, and understands fully that an affair means fun, excitement, no strings, no commitment, and no future together – just sex. The rules need to be worked out before you embark on a physical relationship. It must be made clear that you're going to stay married, and you need acknowledgement from your potential lover that these conditions are acceptable and understood.

Rule 10-Never ever have unprotected sex

I cannot believe the naivety of people when it comes to STDs and unwanted pregnancies. These can certainly be some of the most obvious giveaways. Just because he's had a vasectomy, or she's on the pill or has had a tubal ligation or a hysterectomy, don't assume that everything is safe; these only stop babies, not diseases. Never discount your lover's partner. There are many men who believe that if their lover is married she doesn't pose a risk, but who's to say what her husband gets up to?

The number of one-night stands that end in pregnancy is higher than you would imagine. The same goes for the number of my clients who find out about an affair only after contracting an STD. Therefore protection is literally vital to survival.

Rule 11 - Make calls on your mobile phone at your peril

What would we do without our mobile phones? Well, let me tell you the worst thing any self-respecting cheat can do is use their personal or company mobile phone to conduct an affair. Modern mobiles offer the wife or partner numerous ways in which to trace calls or text messages when there aren't any phone bills to check. Just think of all the opportunities your partner has to check your phone for calls received or made, such as when you're in the shower, mowing the lawns or any time you're asleep. Of course you can always delete all messages and numbers before you get home, put a pin number on the phone, leave it locked in the car or sleep with it, but any or all of these will cause suspicion – so don't.

The solution to this predicament is to buy a prepaid phone and keep it somewhere private. Don't buy the prepaid phone using any form of money card – it's wise to scrape together some cash that can't be traced to a transaction that will appear on a statement. When you buy top-ups don't do it with your credit or eftpos card, as these show up on statements. Always use cash, and withdraw small amounts so large sums don't show up on your statements.

Do remember that no system is foolproof, and it will take just the smallest slip (which is all we need) for your house of cards (because that's what affairs are) to come crashing down.

Rule 12 - Keep your thoughts off paper

When men betray they tend to put their thoughts on paper more often than women do. They often weigh up the pros and cons of the wife and the lover, writing their thoughts down on random pieces of paper that they then leave in a briefcase or office drawer just waiting to be found by a suspicious wife. There are many cases where this has been a man's downfall and has led to him being exposed. It also provides strong ammunition for the wife to use in the face of denial.

Rule 13- The exit plan

This is where all your careful planning should pay off. In all affairs there comes a time when it's over. The reason isn't really important. There will be many – maybe the thrill of the chase has worn off, or the benefits don't exceed the risks of deceit. Whatever the reason the time from now on is crucial to your survival. If you have conducted yourself as I have advised and haven't made outrageous promises that haven't been fulfilled, and if you have been honest with your lover about your expectations, then there is a chance (however slim) that you may survive this affair.

However, we're all only human, and these rules cover the most important aspects of human frailty; breaking just one of them will lead to your downfall. No doubt some of you will try to hold me personally responsible for people flying off in all directions and having affairs. The fact is, you can lead a horse to water but you can't make it drink – and the same is true here.

I've often said that those who choose to betray their partners have a behavioral weakness, arrogance and an "I don't give a shit" kind of attitude. You are either monogamous or you're not. However, one can never lose sight of the fact that it all boils down to choice.

The reason people have affairs is that they consciously choose to do so. No one forces them. So many people use the excuse that it "just happened", but it doesn't just happen. Your clothes don't fall off while you're walking down the street.

Having an affair is something you have to plan and construct, and the very reason you skulk around corners trying not to get caught is because you know it's wrong, but the truth of the matter is that you don't give a shit. So don't try the oldest trick in the book by transferring the blame onto me for bringing this out into the open; take responsibility for your actions and remember that for every action there is a reaction.

Mistresses beware

To all mistresses out there, just bear with me for a while. If you're single and have considered the pros and cons of this liaison, and you have absolutely no expectations and are under no illusions (because this is purely a physical attraction and once the spark goes so will you, without a backward glance), then maybe you will enjoy your fling with your married lover.

But if you're looking for something more and want a future with this man, and you're willing to give your heart to him, then you need to tread very carefully. Just stop for a moment and think of his wife. He's probably told you they've been having problems for some time, maybe that they don't even sleep together any more, and there you are like a breath of fresh air that has entered his life. Let's assume his wife finds out about you, because sooner or later she will. She'll be devastated because she had no idea they were having problems, and as for sleeping in separate rooms – I don't think so. Can you imagine her shock? Well, try, because that's exactly how you will feel in due course. As sure as God made little apples if you stay with this man he will do exactly the same to you.

You need to take a reality check and carefully consider your lover, this married man who's been lying to his wife for as long as you've been involved with him. Why do you believe he's telling you the truth? Just because he says he is? If his life is so bad at home (with no sex, sleeping in the spare room, no communication apart from the occasional argument) then why does he stay there? I'll tell you why – because it's not that bad , or it's not bad at all, but he paints a picture for you and for himself that allows you both to feel these circumstances are valid reasons for betraying his wife.

What if he gave you the following explanation? "Hi, sweetheart, I'm a prick of a guy, I love my wife, I don't want to leave my comfortable home or split my wealth, I'm just a greedy bastard, I don't want to have sex with just one woman so don't think I'm going to fall in love with you. A guy like me has got to do what he wants, when he wants." Now, would you have an affair with this guy? I think not, but if you do, you need to first acknowledge that this is who he really is.

You actually have no idea whether he has had serial dalliances elsewhere during your time with him. Your lover is a liar, so stop being naive and remember: "If he does it with you the chances are he will do it to you."

CHAPTER 13

Women who leave

When Hollywood actress Sandra Bullock found out that her husband of just four years, Jesse James, had been cheating on her, her reaction was very different from that of most women who find themselves in this situation: she left him. Sandra's marriage break-up would have been utterly devastating for her, especially because it was played out in the public eye. But Sandra Bullock had several big advantages: looks, money, profile, and a strong sense of self-worth. Leaving Jesse James would not have been easy, but Sandra obviously decided that staying would have been worse. The sad fact is that 95 per cent of women who are the victims of infidelity stay in their relationships after the betrayal has been discovered. Leaving a relationship can be a long and difficult road, but the rewards far outweigh the pain of staying.

Suzy's story

The event that finally caused the light to dawn for Suzy seems rather insignificant, but when you've been married for over 13 years you get to know your spouse's behavior very well. Even then, it was a long time before Suzy was clear about what was going on, and there was a lot of heartache and stress before she finally decided to take the plunge and take control of her own destiny.

> *My husband, Bob, and I had gone to Wellington for the Christmas break to stay with my parents. It was 10.20 p.m. on Christmas Eve and Bob had gone outside to have a cigarette. I had gone to the bathroom, and through the open window I heard the sound of his mobile phone. A few minutes later I heard him speaking. Strange, I thought,*

that he should be checking the messages on his phone, and even stranger that I should hear him speaking to someone — obviously he had picked up a message and rung the person back. When I asked him about the call he said it was to a colleague from the Wellington office who was wondering if he was coming in over the break. This didn't seem right. If you were waiting for a call, why not leave the phone on all night? It seemed even stranger that Bob should return the call at 10.20 on Christmas Eve when he wouldn't ring a close friend at that time, let alone someone he hardly knew. I was puzzled, and it got me thinking.

Later that night I tried to make sense of what had happened. I started to think about another occurrence one weekend in November when we had called into a petrol station. Bob was paying the bill, and out of boredom I picked up his phone. He had a new job and a new phone which was much smaller than mine. When he saw me with the phone he looked panicky and took it off me, saying, "What are you doing?" I said, "Just looking at it." He quickly checked to make sure the phone was turned off then put it in his pocket. Why the fuss?

On Christmas Day I couldn't shake off the incident from the night before. It just didn't add up. My husband and I were in separate rooms, and while he was in the shower I suddenly felt even more curious and decided to look in his briefcase, where I found his wallet. In it was a receipt for a gold bracelet. How bizarre! Bob had bought me an expensive present for Christmas [which he had managed to forget and leave sitting on the fridge at home] so I found it hard to believe that he would also have bought me a gold bracelet. The date of the receipt was the day before we had bought my present.

The next thing I found [although I very nearly missed it] was a tiny piece of rolled-up paper. On it was a poem that read: "Real love is like a fragile wreck on a storm of emotion. It is all consuming " The only explanation I could come up with was that Bob was having an affair. Perhaps this explained some of the other unusual things that had happened over the last few months. Bob had been coming home late an awful lot, and whenever I tried to phone him after work his mobile was turned off. There had also been a lot of so-called games of golf during the week and the weekends. On several occasions I was dead certain he hadn't played golf at all. This included a Sunday morning when he had got up about 9 a.m. and declared, "I'm off to golf." He had discussed golf with a friend earlier in the week and they had realized there was a tournament on that weekend and the course would be closed to everyone else.

"But I thought the course was closed?" I said. "I just rang the course and they said if I turned up after 11 I could play," Bob replied. "But who will you play with?" I asked. "I'll just make up a foursome when I get there," he said. That, too, was very unusual. I wasn't convinced, so when he had gone I decided to press the redial button on the phones. None of them reached the golf club – they were all numbers we had called the previous evening. As well as that, Bob kept ringing in at various times during the morning and early afternoon saying he would be home shortly. He finally turned up at about 4 o'clock, and his feet didn't stink and there was no mud on his trousers,

even though it was a drizzly day. When I asked him about this, he couldn't explain it.

So, on Christmas Day presents were exchanged, but no gold bracelet ! He couldn't possibly have left that behind as well, could he? Later that morning we went for a walk. Bob had seemed a bit twitchy all morning, and finally I took a deep breath and said, "What's going on? What are you up to?" He looked startled and said, "Nothing. I'm not up to anything." "What about the phone call last night?" I asked; "I find it very hard to believe you would ring a colleague so late on Christmas Eve. You're definitely up to something." But he managed to change the subject and I let it drop.

From then on my senses were heightened and I watched Bob like a hawk. Every morning he would get up early and go out for a cigarette. His phone hardly ever left his side yet it was never turned on. Even when he was sitting outside reading a book, the phone went with him. I started checking his phone each morning when he was in the shower to see if it would ring when I turned it on. It never did. Then one day I borrowed his phone to ring a friend in Auckland and hit the redial button by mistake. Six numbers flashed up, and I thought it was a phone number. I tried ringing the number but it didn't work. As I thought more about it I suddenly realized that the first four numbers were only one different from the PIN numbers on everything else he had. It dawned on me that the last two numbers were 1 and 7 – 1 to access a message and 7 to clear it. Aha, I had cracked it. He had changed his PIN number so I wouldn't be able to access his messages !

From then on, I checked his phone every morning, but

again there were no messages. It finally dawned on me that he was clearing his messages before his cigarette, so by the time I got to the phone they had all been deleted. But still the phone was glued to his pocket, and on one occasion when we were visiting relatives he took it outside and turned it on. It rang ! He listened to the message, which took some minutes, then, looking very sheepish; he called up to me and told me to remind him to ring so-and-so at work the next day. Rubbish ! There was no way in the world that I believed it was a work colleague. The next day we had dinner with friends, and again the damn phone came along. I joked several times that Bob was waiting for his girlfriend to ring and he just laughed.

On the drive back to my parents' house he said to me, "You think I'm having an affair, don't you?" "Yes, I do," I said. "Well, I'm not!" he replied. I told him there was no other way I could make sense of some of the things that had been happening lately. I still hadn't told him about finding the bracelet receipt or the poem. When he arrived home he put his arms round me and said, "Don't give up on me just yet." I looked him in the eye and said, "Can you swear to me on your mother's grave that you are not or have not been having an affair?" To which he replied, "I swear."

My Christmas was totally ruined. When we got back home I was determined to get to the bottom of things. We arrived home late so I decided to get to that phone first thing in the morning. I woke at about six and shot downstairs and turned on the phone. It rang immediately: "You have two messages!" The first message was from a woman, who said that she had rather been hoping he would pick up the phone this time as it was really hard just leaving messages and not being able to hear his voice / The second message, in the same voice, announced that it was "Secret Squirrel", then she described how her trip with "the other three" was going, and how she missed him terribly and couldn't wait to catch up with him again in a few days I was floored. I sat at the kitchen table shaking as I felt the blood drain out of my face. It was all true. Everything I had thought and suspected was true. Everything he had said was a lie. And I had been trying desperately to give him the benefit of the doubt. I sat downstairs for about half an hour before going upstairs and banging around the bedroom to wake him up.

"Can't you keep the noise down?" he said.

"After the week I've just had, what do you expect?" I replied.

"Not this again."

"So, you still maintain that you're not having an affair," I hissed.

"No, I'm not," he said.

"Well, you're a liar. I just cleared two phone messages from "Secret Squirrel", so don't give me that rubbish."

At this, he went into shock. I started flinging all sorts of questions at him and he just clammed up. I referred back to a business trip he had taken in November when he had driven down to New Plymouth and Palmerston North.

"Did she go with you?" I demanded.

"No, absolutely not!" he shouted back. I later found out

that was yet another lie and that she had in fact gone with him.

Bob got himself out of bed, headed outside, and started smoking from what appeared to be every orifice in his body. I hit him with a barrage of questions and demanded to know who she was. Finally he said her name was Jane, and then he told me where she lived. I felt totally devastated. I just couldn't believe this was happening.

He then proceeded to tell me that he had met her at work, and that she had rung him up after he had left and started a new job. She wanted him to help her find a new job, so they had met for a drink and it had started from there. This, too, was a lie. They had actually hooked up at a farewell function at work. He also said he had been trying to call it off, but that she wouldn't let go or take no for an answer. I told him it was very easy to get rid of someone if you really wanted to, but that if you continued to give them air time there was no way they would get the message. He just said that she kept ringing him and turning up at his work in the morning and hanging around the car park. He also said she was "unbalanced" and continued to make derogatory remarks about her, insisting that he was trying to get rid of her. He then offered the information that she would probably call that evening, as it was New Year's Eve.

I didn't know what to do, and whether to stay or leave. I felt as if I had to work it through on my own before telling anyone else. All through the day I kept asking Bob why it had happened, what I had done wrong, how he could lie to me like that – but he couldn't give me any answers. I wanted to know everything about her, but he kept put-

ting her down. Was this supposed to impress me? Did he think this would make me feel better? It made me feel sick. He had risked our marriage for someone he said was "a slapper" with a reputation at work as long as your arm. He even said she had tried to sleep with most of the men at work and that she had bragged about other affairs she had had. Nice girl!

On the first day of work after the holidays, I rang her. I told her how disgusted I was and that Bob had told me the whole story. I said he was trying to get rid of her and that he didn't wish to see her anymore. I also said that she could return the bracelet.

Sure enough, at about six that night I saw a car drive past, and a few seconds later this creature walked towards me with an envelope clutched in her hand. I confronted her at the gate. She appeared to be about 23 or 24 – turns out she was almost 30. Bob was 11 years older than her. She was about my height but of slimmer build, and was wearing a striped sundress that came to about six inches above her knees. She was nothing like what I had expected.

The next day Bob told me that Jane had turned up outside his work in tears, wanting an explanation. He said he had told her it was all off, and that she was very upset. He would not see her again, he told me. If she rang he would hang up on her, and if she arrived at his work he would walk away. He said he wanted us to work things out and for me to be able to trust him again.

About a week later, we were sitting watching TV when Bob looked at me and asked, "What's wrong with you?"

"What's wrong?" I replied. "You must be joking."

"Aren't you over it yet?" he asked.

This from a man who would get jealous if I so much as mentioned the name of a man from my past or someone he didn't know. He would always sneer, "An old boyfriend, eh?" Had the boot been on the other foot and I been the one having the affair, he would have gone ballistic and my life would have been hell.

He seemed to think that because he had said it was over, it should also be over for me. I could think of nothing else, every waking minute of the day. It never left me. Every time he was out of my sight I wondered where he was and whether or not he was with her. Every time the phone rang, I wondered if it would be her. My mind worked overtime as I went back over incidents that had happened in the past.

February arrived and still I had my doubts that the affair was over. Then one Saturday afternoon I received a call from a man called Jack, who said he was Jane's husband. He said that we needed to talk. I met him the following day and he told me he was fairly certain that Jane and Bob were going to "give it a go" and move in together. He said that Jane had told him she had met Bob the previous day, when Bob had told me he was playing golf. I replied that Bob had never mentioned anything to me about leaving, but if he really wanted to go I wasn't going to stop him; in fact, I was going to suggest he do just that.

Later I confronted Bob, and he said he had no plans to

leave, that it was all in Jane's imagination. I told him it was a pretty wild assumption for her to make and that he must have said something to give her that idea. I added that if he wanted to leave, he should do so now. He said that he didn't want to go, and that everything Jack had said was rubbish.

This situation continued for some time, until finally one morning Jack turned up at our house. He said that Bob had been seeing Jane again, and that it had to stop. Bob continued to insist that the relationship was over and that he had no intention of leaving me for Jane.

By now I was feeling desperate and didn't know what I should do. Bob kept telling me I was nuts and paranoid, and that it was just my dirty little mind playing tricks on me. I needed to know for certain what was going on, because I figured that if I wasn't nuts yet, I soon would be. I had previously scanned the phone book to see if there were any private investigators listed, though I couldn't imagine where I would begin. The thought of ringing a strange man and telling him my story was all a bit much. It had never occurred to me that there might be a female investigator until I came across Julia's name. I still wasn't sure what I was going to say, and I thought she would probably tell me I was nuts too, but I really needed someone else to take this thing away from me. I didn't want to discuss it with any of my friends or my family, so I rang Julia. She didn't think I was nuts – in fact, not only did she say she had heard a lot of it before, but she also said she had experienced something similar herself. I gave her as many details as I could, and we agreed to meet the next day.

Julia sure didn't look like a private investigator. Not a grubby raincoat in sight. I gave her all the information I had – phone numbers, number plates, photos, descriptions, and all the background I could. She said she would start the next day. Bob had said he was going to a meeting at another branch of his company, so we decided that Julia would watch him. She got to the offices before Bob, and saw him arrive and park his car. At about noon Bob rang me and said that he was going to be there for another hour or so, then he would return to his own office. I immediately rang Julia and relayed this information, and she said she could see Bob – he had just made a call and was now getting in his car and driving off. So much for being in the meeting for another hour. Julia followed for a distance but unfortunately lost him on the motorway. She then rang Jane's work, and was told she had gone to lunch.

By now I was pretty wound up about everything and found it almost impossible to keep quiet about what I knew. Bob started to get wind of me, and said, "If you don't believe me, why don't you have me followed?" "Don't tempt me," I replied. I also made the mistake of ringing him frequently to check up on where he was. I should have stayed well out of it, but it's very difficult when it's in your face and someone keeps telling you that you are wrong.

The next day Julia sat outside Jane's work and waited. Bob told me he was off to the same branch again at 12.30, and I passed the information on to Julia. Sure enough, Jane popped her head out the door at 12.30 and scooted off down the road, preening all the way. She made a brief stop at a wine shop, and came out with a brown paper bag twisted at the top. Julia later described the next few minutes as like being in a Formula One motor race as Jane dashed off at breakneck speed, lane-hopping and weaving in and out of traffic with no regard for her own or anyone else's safety. Her speed reached 100 mph before she cut across three lanes of traffic and dived down a slip road. Julia, for her own safety and to remain within the law, eased off but managed to keep her within sight, until Jane turned off and wove her way through some back streets, which she seemed to know quite well, before disappearing from view. Julia and her team checked on all Bob's haunts and a number of motels in the area but neither he nor Jane could be found.

I knew I would hear from Bob, and sure enough, a couple of hours later he rang and said he'd had a very strange call from Jane saying she had been followed at lunchtime. I told him I couldn't talk at the moment and would call him later. Ten minutes later he rang back demanding to know whether I had had Jane followed. I denied this.

When I arrived home that evening Bob was asleep. I woke him and, looking very sheepish, he said he couldn't understand what the call from Jane was all about. I asked him when he had got the call and where she had telephoned from. He said she had called from work at 12.30. Well, I knew that couldn't be so – she was leaving work at that time. He then said that he had not met her that day.

I started going through his pockets, and in one of his jackets I found a cassette tape. It was clearly labeled in what Looked Like a woman's handwriting, and was entitled "Stolen Secret Moments". The titles of the songs were all written out – they were all suggestive, soppy titles Like

"She's a Mixed Up Shook Up Girl", "Up Where We Belong" and "Without You". I assumed Jane had given it to him that day, but when I tackled him about it he went berserk and said he had had it for ages. When I asked why it was in his pocket he said it had been in his golf bag, and he had only decided to move it that day. I didn't believe him.

I then admitted that I had had him followed, and that I knew he had met Jane that day. He said I didn't know that, and demanded to know where they had gone if I knew the truth. Of course, I didn't know exactly. He had called my bluff. I told him she had bought a bottle of wine at Lunchtime, and he said he knew nothing about that and perhaps she had met someone else.

The following day I managed to locate his phone records for the previous month, and when I looked at them I almost died. During that one month he had made 67 calls and spoken for over 400 minutes. I made a copy and decided to tackle Bob when he came home. I told him he didn't have a relationship with Jane, but an obsession. His reply was that I should see how many calls she had made to him – in most cases, he said, he was returning her calls.

When I analyzed the calls more closely I found that a lot of them had been made to her work number out of hours when all he would have got was her voice mail. He had confessed some months back that one way in which they had communicated was by his Leaving and clearing messages on her voice mail. He knew her PIN number but he didn't have his own voice mail. I checked every number he had rung and one of them turned out to be a motel in the area Julia had searched the previous day. It seemed Bob and Jane had used this motel on another occasion.

Later that afternoon Jane rang, wanting to speak to Bob. He said he didn't want to speak to her, but about an hour later there was a knock at the door. It was Jane. She said she wanted to clear things up. I told her to get Lost, but Bob persuaded me to let her in and hear what she had to say. How dare he? They sat there chatting like old friends! She then told me she had not met Bob the previous day, and when I asked her about the wine she said I had it wrong – she had bought a bottle of lemonade and a sausage roll from the dairy next door. I knew that was rubbish, since Julia had been very clear about it. Then Jane said that she and Bob were not seeing each other, and that their relationship was well and truly over.

Later Bob confessed that he had seen Jane over the last few months but that he had been trying to get rid of her. He said she kept ringing him up all the time, and if he hung up on her she would simply ring back. He promised that he really wasn't going to see her again but, as I pointed out, I had heard this many times before.

Over the next two weeks Bob spent some time away for his work, both in Australia and also down country. While he was in Australia I had his mobile, and I received a number of hang-up calls, which I assumed were from Jane. Bob told me he received several calls at work and in his hotel room in Australia, and each time he would tell her to get lost and hang up. I told him that the situation had become ridiculous and that we should consult a lawyer. He agreed.

The next week we met with a lawyer and applied for a protection order against Jane. She had obviously lost the plot and there was no telling what she would do. Two days later, Bob received a package in the mail at work. When he opened it up it contained a piece of red satin, and inside that were cuttings from her hair with a note saying something about the strands of hair reflecting the way he had savagely cut her from his life. I went straight back to the lawyer and the court granted a temporary protection order on the grounds that she was unstable, at the same time ordering her to undergo anger management counseling.

Bob and I decided to try and work things out, and a year later Jane was gone from our lives, we had a six-week-old baby, and all was reasonably well. I could hardly believe that it had all happened – it seems like a pathetic soap opera.

I know you'll be asking why I stayed and put up with all the crap for so long. It's not that easy to explain, and I'm not sure I totally understand it myself. I have always taken my marriage very seriously and I found the idea of picking up sticks and Leaving after 13 years very hard. It was also incredibly hard to believe that the person who was supposed to be my best friend could lie to me and treat me that way. I kept accepting his explanations because I really wanted to believe them in spite of the fact that my common sense was telling me otherwise. That was why I had to prove or disprove what I suspected – I didn't want to make a mistake and walk out purely on the grounds on my suspicions.

At the time, Julia kept me sane, and I only wish I had con-

tacted her a lot sooner. It was such a relief to share the problem with someone who didn't think I was nuts and imagining everything. I also realize now that she would have had a much better chance of catching Bob and Jane together had I not in my anger and frustration spilt the beans and let them in on my secret weapon. This should be a lesson to anyone else in a similar position.

What I learnt from this episode in my life was that I should always trust my instincts because they are generally correct? If I had been able to put Bob on "mute" – taking away his words and just looking at his actions – I would have seen it all more clearly.

After a year a lot of my anger had gone, but I knew the disappointment would probably always be there. I was under no illusions about what Bob had done. He was totally responsible for his actions. He had this affair because he wanted to. He may not have set out to start it, but he didn't prevent it either. And though he said he kept trying to get rid of Jane, his actions didn't say that. He not only kept it going, he encouraged it. He was flattered by the attention, and the male ego is a force to be reckoned with.

Well, to fast-forward ten years, I did eventually leave Bob. I hung around for another four years before walking out the door with two children, both under five. The defining moment came when Bob accused me of having an affair and a little switch went off inside my head. I remember the incident very clearly, and thinking what am I doing here? What's in it for me? We had been married for almost 20 years and I had endured affairs [oh, yes, I found out about some more, and I still keep hearing stor-

ies], verbal abuse, lies and threats. I turned to Bob and said, "That's it. I'm out of here."

It took me another eight months to actually go, but once I had left I never wavered. This was a horrible time, perhaps even worse than the time when Jane was around, but it was worth it. The first night I spent alone in my new bed in my new home was amazing. My friends said I looked like a different person once I'd left – as though the world had been lifted from my shoulders.

I've been on my own now for six years and have never regretted leaving. I no longer have to worry about where he is, what he's doing or who he's doing it with. I don't have to suffer the put downs and abuse or outbursts of rage.

I'm not saying it has been easy raising two young children on my own, and at times it's been hard financially, but any worries have been far outweighed by no longer having to deal with the emotional stress of living with Bob. I know there are a lot of women who won't leave their marriages because they are afraid of the unknown. I don't have much time for women who complain that they couldn't possibly cope without the money coming in. Get a grip, girls, and stop being doormats!

Women can be their own worst enemies. We leave school, get token jobs and then end up marrying men who either have money or have the ability to earn good money, and then we don't take any interest or responsibility for managing our finances. We leave it up to them. Fortunately I didn't do that. I always paid the bills. Women need to be aware of what goes on with the family finances and *actively participate in bill paying and financial matters. Doing this gives you much more strength if things do turn to custard and you have to start again on your own. And if you need some help there are also seminars available to women to empower them with these skills – people like Julia can advise you about these.*

On the flip side, I believe men are also their own worst enemies. They flaunt their money and status to capture the trophy wife or partner, then complain bitterly when it turns sour and the women go for their dough! Wasn't that what they used for bait in the first place?

Having left Bob, I have a much better life. I have the freedom to do what I like, and I don't feel as though I have to compromise my standards. I take a much deeper interest in the way people behave than I used to, and I don't jump into friendships without first getting to know the other person. I can see where I went wrong when I hooked up with Bob, and I can now recognize the same traits in other people. Getting to know someone takes time, and my advice to anyone reading this would be to slow down and not be in a hurry to take the plunge.

And, an important point, trust your instincts. As I said before, my instincts have always been very good – better than I realized. I had doubts about Bob from the beginning but I couldn't explain them. The fact is, it doesn't matter that I couldn't. If I get these feelings now, I tread very carefully. I am usually right in some way or another.

The other thing women worry about is of course their kids. Well, my children are doing really well. I don't believe that it would have been better for the children had I stayed, and there is plenty of evidence from those in the know to back this up. It has always got to be better for children to live in a house with one parent who is happy than to live with two parents who either don't speak to each other or are constantly arguing. I hear stories all the time about how children are seriously affected emotionally by the stress that arises from living with warring parents. Don't do this to your kids, and don't use them as an excuse to stay. Have the courage to stand up and do what you know is the right thing. Your friends and family will help and support you. Trust me, I know.

CHAPTER 14

Most frequently asked questions

If he wants her so much why does he stay with me?

Because he doesn't want her more than he wants you, he just wants her as well as you. If he's fallen head over heels in love with this woman and he can't live without her then he might leave you for her, as some men do. The ones who don't are just plain greedy; they want the whole cake, not just a slice. If you've only recently found out about the affair then you can see why he hasn't had to leave you — he's been having the best of both worlds without having to make sacrifices such as splitting the assets and losing face among his friends. Mostly these men play and stay because their wives let them.

Is it wrong to have him watched if I suspect him of having an affair?

Absolutely not. Don't ever feel guilty about protecting yourself. As his wife you have every right to know what he's doing with your health, finances and emotions. I get so angry with women who say they feel guilty about having their husbands watched when they suspect he's betraying them. Ask yourself: did he feel guilty about disrespecting you, about lying to you and consciously hurting you? No, he didn't, so if you are smart you won't feel guilty about trying to find out the truth.

Why does he keep doing this to me? What sort of man is he?

He keeps doing it to you because you let him, and the only explanation for this sort of man is that he's an uncaring, immature, selfish bastard. A child of four or five wants what he wants when he wants it, but a grown man should have learned right from wrong and clearly these men haven't. In fact, I'm doing real men a disservice by calling these guys "men" because quite clearly they aren't. However, if you don't respect yourself you can't expect your husband to. And if you're one of those women who scream and shout but don't take any action, remember you can't keep doing the same thing and expect a different result.

By action I don't mean making an appointment for him to see a counselor, because that won't work unless he does it off his own bat. He has to show he's willing to stick it out and not go two or three times and think, "Hey presto! I'm cured." If he isn't willing to do this, and you're not prepared to up the ante, then expect to continue living a life of emotional turmoil.

He's lied to me so much. How can I ever trust what he says again?

This is one of the hardest questions, because there is no one answer. To learn to trust someone again after something as devastating as infidelity is extremely hard and in some cases impossible. It is such an individual choice, and only you will know if you feel truly comfortable with what is being said and done.

If your partner is willing to be completely open and hi e nothing from you then in essence he must be completely predictable and be prepared to be patient with you. Then there is a chance for you to restore trust in the relationship. But because we know trust has to be earned, it can be a long, long road back. There's no quick fix for infidelity. In fact, it can take literally years to restore trust.

Many men believe that once they have confessed, that should be the end of it and they don't feel they have to do any more. But let me tell you that unless you know that you've been heard on all levels and your partner has understood the gravity of his immaturity and the choices he's made, then you'll never get over his infidelity. You may as well divide up the assets now.

I know he's having a relationship, but is it sexual?

Of course it's sexual. Do fish swim? You would have to have rocks in your head to honestly believe that someone engaging in an affair is just going out for coffee or dinner because affairs are all about sex, not sitting around drinking coffee.

It doesn't matter if it's looking at either print or internet pornography, chatting with other women in chat rooms, or physically having an affair, because the end desire is sex. If it was all so innocent then the only question you would have to ask your partner would be, "Would you do any or all of these things with me present?" Then there would be no need for such elaborate lies. If it's not sexual then he should be able to say: "I'm having coffee with such and such a person," and in doing so be comfortable if you were to join them.

The very reason your partner lies to you either blatantly or by omission is because he knows what he's doing is wrong. When you ask the question "Is it sexual?" what you're doing is trying to justify your partner's deception and minimize your emotional anguish.

Is it my fault?

How can it be your fault if you didn't know it was happening? You didn't give it your stamp of approval so how could you stop it? However, if it has happened before then you have to take responsibility for your part. What you may find is that the reason you ask this question is that your husband has tried to shift the blame by telling you that if you were only more attentive, less busy, slimmer etc., etc., etc., he would never have done this. Do not take any of that on board. For every action there is a reaction, and maybe he should start to take responsibility for his actions.

Why won't he stop when he sees how much it hurts me?

The reason he hurts you is because he doesn't care – he doesn't respect you, he's self-centered and selfish. He shows you by his actions how he really feels towards you, and no amount of talking can make it otherwise. If you want him to stop, then stand up for yourself. Show him it's not acceptable and mean it.

I think my husband's having an affair but he's at home each evening, so how can he be?

This doesn't surprise me because many affairs are conducted during the day. This happens mostly when both parties are married and to go out in the evening would arouse suspicion. However, if the woman is single this is when you may notice the odd late night or even a bogus business trip because she's far more flexible than a married woman. Many of my clients seem to think affairs are about long languid afternoons together, but in my experience they're much more likely to be just snatched moments during the day and it's all over and done within half an hour. Remember that time isn't the issue here; this is all about sex.

Why won't he tell me the truth? That's all I ask.

I wish I had a dollar for every time I've heard this. You'll probably never know the reasons why, but in the vast majority of cases the husband is a gutless bastard and his lies are to avoid what he knows will be an unpleasant time if he tells you the truth. He hopes (because it often works) that if he denies and denies it will go away and you'll give up asking. His lies can also be a protection against you, in that if he tells you the truth he may feel threatened that you will use the information to undermine him or take control of the relationship. And finally, he may fear that there will be far-reaching consequences with family and work colleagues which will damage his image in the eyes of others. When he knows that you know the truth and he still blatantly lies, there is no excuse and no justification. There is therefore no way you're ever going to be able to make a liar tell the truth.

If I don't catch him in the act won't he just say it didn't happen?

You'll probably never get the evidence you think you need (a photograph of your partner in the sexual act) but you will get all the evidence you need in order to confront your partner and make a decision based on his responses. When it comes to confrontation you must plan carefully what you're going to say. Firstly, you need to clearly identify what information has been gathered and also how your husband's story contradicts what's been said before. If, for instance, your husband has been seen entering a hotel room with a woman at 11o'clock at night and doesn't emerge until the next day and then, when confronted, denies anything happened and continues to deny, then he's showing you his absolute disregard for you. There's no point in wasting your energies in trying to elicit an honest response.

How can I stop him continually cheating on me?

There is absolutely nothing YOU can do to stop him. Only he can change his behavior – not you. As I've said many times before: "Leopards don't change their spots and frogs don't turn into princes." If you're living with a serial betrayer the only thing you can do to ensure he doesn't do it again is to remove yourself from the situation.

Why do you need to know who the other person is when it's a 50/50 split nowadays and adultery has gone out of the window as grounds for divorce?

Initially needing to know has nothing to do with money and everything to do with uncovering deceit, because no one likes to be lied to and especially not by their spouse. Knowing has everything to do with putting your life back in order and being able to make choices about your future. Uncovering emotional deceit often leads to uncovering financial deceit; for example, if the husband has been financially supporting or lavishing gifts and trips on his mistress using matrimonial funds that are not solely his to use. That's when needing to know has everything to do with money.

Should I stay for the children and the family unit?

Children always pick up on any tension at home, and can blame themselves for what's going on especially when parents are fighting. So I would say one happy parent is better than two warring parents.

When I say I'm going to leave, why does my partner not take me seriously?

Because you haven't left yet. Threats without any action are just that: empty threats.

CHAPTER 15

Turn the wounds into wisdom

Prevention is better than cure

You can't go around giving every new person you meet a lie-detector test — as much as you might like to. After you've experienced infidelity it takes time to trust yourself in order to trust someone else, and serial philanderers are hardly likely to admit their true nature to you. So in order to protect yourself when you first meet someone it's essential to be a little guarded, especially in the beginning.

Ask questions about his past relationships. Has he been married in the past? What caused his marriage to end? How many serious relationships has he had? Take note of how he answers. If you don't feel comfortable with his answers, don't ignore your intuition. Maybe his friends and family could shed some light.

Observe how he behaves when you're out together, especially in female company. A lot of philanderers can't keep their eyes to themselves. We know it is nom1al and healthy to have an appreciation of the opposite sex, but there's a line between appreciation and disrespect for the person you are with.

Secrecy is another giveaway for the philanderer, but don't confuse secrecy with privacy. Everyone has private zones and that's perfectly normal. Secrets, on the other hand, are things you must keep hidden, and they may have the potential to destroy your relationship. That's why betrayal is always secret. If you have sex with someone outside your marriage then that's not private, that's a secret. It's not about "I can't tell you," it's about "I won't tell you."

Philanderers are more often than not very charming, with the gift of the gab, and always know exactly what a woman wants to hear. They are usually pretty accomplished in the bedroom department as well, but you might well ask if the act is sincere. The answer is no, it's exactly that, an act. Philanderers have mastered the art of seduction for their own selfish mean s. They have no regard for anyone else, only for getting what they want when they want and from whomever they can.

Have you ever noticed how quickly people pass judgment on others, especially if someone is charming and shows them even the slightest kindness, in which case the judgment is always a favorable one? Serial killers can have moments of kindness but you wouldn't want to be married to one. Most people will have an opinion and make an assumption with virtually no evidence at all, and that's without any form of emotional attachment. So what hope is there for us to be objective when our hearts are involved?

Have you ever heard a woman say after her husband has left her for another woman: "I feel as though I don't even know who he is any more"? That's probably because she chose to overlook many vital signs and clues to his personality in the beginning. When choosing a mate you need to weigh up all the information as you gather it and see if it corresponds to what you're seeing and hearing. Listen and learn all you can about the subject of your affection. Don't feel guilty about doing a thorough job when in fact it's the most sensible approach to take. Look at it as being lovingly suspicious.

When you first meet someone, especially through the internet, personal ads or contact magazines, you don't have a clue about their emotional or financial history. It's not as though they come with bona fide documents showing you that what they say is correct, so you have to trust but be aware. You don't know if this person who has caught your attention has a criminal record, children dotted all over the place, has been abusive to women in the past or is a health risk. You only know what he tells you.

I'm astounded by the number of clients who say to me after the love of their life has betrayed them (either emotionally by cheating or financially by conning them out of thousands of dollars), "He was so charming." Well, he's not exactly going to show you his true colors when he has a hidden agenda, is he?

This is where I'm going to repeat myself. Don't assume that because someone says all the right things in the beginning he must be a good person. Don't take everything you hear at face value, especially when you don't know someone.

When you buy a used car you don't believe everything the salesman tells you, because you don't know him and therefore you don't know if he is telling the truth. That's why you get an independent mechanic to check the car over – just to be on the safe side. That's being smart, so why is it that people feel guilty if they even consider doing the same thing to someone they've just met?

I can understand that you might feel all this caution goes against how you were brought up; that is, to treat others as you would want to be treated yourself. Unfortunately, not everyone is like that. That's the problem, and one of our biggest mistakes is in believing that they are. The world is a very different place now from when our parents were growing up and there are some people who have absolutely no regard for anyone else's feelings. I'm not saying you have to become cynical, because you don't, but if you learn to first look and listen and not just assume, you'll be able to spot pretty quickly someone who isn't on the level. Just be alert and see if there are any clues, because as I've said before, people always show you who they are in the beginning. Never overlook your intuition. Unless it screams at you that you can trust this person, go slowly and take your time.

Making assumptions can often lead to bad judgments. There are certain people in society we automatically look up to because we assume they're worthy of our esteem. Most of us have been guilty of accepting without question the word of doctors, lawyers, priests, judges and others in positions of authority. These people have enormous power to abuse because of the simple fact that they appear the least likely to do so. In my line of work I come across many professional men with more kinks than a corrugated-iron roof. Just because someone has achieved a high level of education and learning doesn't make them immune to being emotional deceivers.

There is a raft of questions to be considered before choosing a mate.

Here's a good analogy: if you wanted a dog and were a responsible person you would very carefully choose the dog to suit your lifestyle. If you lived in a small inner-city apartment you wouldn't get a Great Dane, and if you were a farmer with 5000 head of sheep you wouldn't get a Chihuahua as a sheepdog. Instead, you would look for a dog of a size and temperament to suit the situation.

It's not that different from choosing a mat e. There are women who will make out at the beginning of a relationship that they love sport. They'll go with their new partner to the rugby or soccer, cricket or motor racing when in actual fact the reason for tagging along is to curry favor with their partner.

The minute they're married their interest in sport is turned off like a tap and they don't go any more – they've got the guy; they no longer have to pretend. This is misrepresentation and can cause problems further down the track as the guy hasn't got what he thought he was getting. The old adage "Love will conquer all" doesn't appear to be working in the real world. If it were, there wouldn't be the number of relationships in crisis that there are.

Most people have a list of requirements when looking for a mate, but they often overlook the essentials. Some women go shopping for a man with a very limited list of requirements, yet when shopping for a single dress those very same women will try on at least 15 different ones before making a choice. Often, they simply require their prospective partner to have money, power and a university education, which I guess puts Bill Gates out of the running as far as the education goes. Then there are guys who stipulate that the woman they're looking for must be under 35 with no children, so I guess that rules out Angelina Jolie as well.

Can you see how narrow-minded these requirements are and how unrealistic, but more importantly, how limiting they can be? If we choose our mate on such terms then the narrowness of the criteria must surely increase the chances of making the wrong choice.

Through my work I find that many women feel like beggars rather than choosers when it comes to finding a mate. Some feel an enormous relief when anyone shows an interest in them because they've convinced themselves, for whatever reason (maybe they are just lonely or feel too old), that no one is going to want them. They hope to be chosen rather than believe they have the opportunity to choose. What they should be doing is concentrating on what they really want and need at this point in their lives by doing some work on themselves and developing who they are so they don't just get on the bus because it stops at their place.

Make choices based on what you want; don't just accept what's there. So many of the women I work for find themselves tied up with deadbeat, drop-kick, good-for-nothing men. These women welcome them into their homes, their hearts, their lives and their bank accounts. They wouldn't normally choose men like this, but then they didn't, they just accepted what came along. If you feel grateful to be the chosen one then you can't be particularly choosy. And that's why many of my clients find themselves the victims of emotional and financial fraud.

If you feel a desperate need for an attachment to a man and to be loved, it first has to come from within you. There will always be droughts in your romantic life, but isn't it better to tough them out so you know exactly what you want and who you are, and know that you don't need a relationship with a man (any man) to make you complete and more fulfilled? This is why many of the women I deal with complain bitterly when they've been deceived, because they didn't get to know or really care who he was to begin with. Do you really think the true man of your dreams would want a desperate woman?

The reason 95 per cent of my female clients stay in marriages where they have been betrayed is that they just accept betrayal as part and parcel of married life. They stay, if the truth be told, out of fear, dependency and a desire for security.

Part of the reason for my writing this book is the sheer frustration I feel when I hear over and over again from women whose husbands have lied, cheated, deceived and destroyed them, "But I still love him." Believe me, this isn't love. This is hanging on to a fantasy, a dream of what you thought you had, not what you've ended up with.

I don't think there is a man alive who would tolerate the behavior many of my clients accept. Women will make compromises that can have serious effects on their physical, emotional, mental and financial self in return for moments of happiness. I am staggered at how intelligent women accept appalling behavior from the man who promised to love and cherish them. Love is about respect, admiration, commitment, honesty and trust, none of which these men are showing these women, and yet I keep hearing: "I know he cheated on me and said some terribly hurtful things and will probably do it again, but I still love him."

It's incredible how women who are married to professionals with social standing will endure in silence because they care more about what other people are going to think than about valuing themselves. They believe there is a certain social stigma attached to once having been the wife of so-and-so but now just being themselves.

I remember reading many years ago about the ex-wife of Roger Moore and how terribly hurt she felt because everyone in their old group of showbiz friends ignored her when she was no longer married to Roger. If you put that much value on what other people think I suppose you deserve what you get. It all comes down to this, and I can't emphasize it enough: if you don't value yourself, love yourself or put a high enough price tag on yourself then you will only get what you believe you are worth. As the mother of three daughters let me ask you this: would you want your daughters to have a husband who was a lying, cheating, self-centered, immature, arrogant bastard?. You don't have to answer. So why is it OK for you? And why is it OK for you to send that message to your daughters?

There are times when I wish I had a magic wand and could make the hurt disappear but that would defeat the purpose. The hurt is there for a reason, and the reason is to teach us a lesson in this lifetime, otherwise we don't grow. I feel this way especially about women I encounter who've been widowed after long marriages and get tied up with a love rat, or women whose husbands just up and go off into the sunset with a different model (notice I don't say better or younger because that's not accurate) after 30 or 40 years together. These women are like inexperienced kids when it comes to distinguishing between romance, love, intimacy and sex.

Elizabeth and Fran, two clients who have confused sex with intimacy, come to mind. Both women were in their sixties and financially secure, and both had nursed their husbands through long illnesses to their final days. What happened in each case is clear. Elizabeth and Fran had very human needs. They needed to be connected to and feel close to someone again. However, these women were confusing what they were getting with what they wanted. Both had been married to good honest men, therefore they assumed that because the new men who entered their lives appeared kind and showed interest in them, they were good men too.

Women fantasize about romance, and in their minds they turn a sexual encounter into a romantic one and assume their partner does as well. But as we know, sex for men is often just that, and doesn't include romance, which is exactly what happened here. These two women felt that because their men had sex with them the relationship had moved to another level of intimacy, but as I pointed out so eloquently, dung beetles have sex so don't go confusing it with anything more than that.

Intimacy is about being able to talk about anything and

everything, and being able to talk freely about what you're doing, what you want and what you don't want. When I asked Elizabeth some routine questions about her man it turned out she effectively knew nothing about him, although in her mind she felt she did, so much so that she was starting to have thoughts of a long-term relationship.

Women like Elizabeth and Fran probably have more excuse than most because both come from a generation that simply didn't discuss intimate and personal issues (and because younger women today have a lot more sexual experience). To them sex was a precious gift to be given with love and not something given away casually. They assumed that their new partners understood the value of the gift and felt the same way.

There are plenty of women who jump into bed with someone they hardly know on the first date and then beat themselves up afterwards because they never see or hear from him again. If they took time to clarify a few of the finer points before jumping head first into bed then they wouldn't have to beat themselves up because there would be no misunderstanding and they wouldn't feel used. This behavior is using sex to get love and women do it all the time; and men use this behavior to get sex. Can you blame them if it's gift-wrapped?

In Fran's case, she allowed sex to happen far too soon in order to camouflage her feelings of loneliness and her need for closeness. Women like this are starving but they're looking for sustenance from someone else in the form of what they feel is intimacy and caring, but instead it's only sex. The man who came into Fran's life was a con man. He only came at all because Fran called him to clean her windows, and the fact that she had paid him was immaterial in her eyes because she had romanticized the situation out of all proportion simply because they'd had sex.

Just as women take words far too literally, they also take a man showing sexual interest to mean more than it does. Don't give sex undeserved power. Yes, it can be fantastic and sublime when it's with the right person, but don't use it to fill a void of emptiness and loneliness in your life, because it never works for longer than the moment lasts.

Respect, trust, love and commitment

So, in essence, never say never; don't say you will never trust anyone again or that you will never get involved with anyone again. Don't lock your heart and happiness away in isolation. We all have a core purpose for being in this world and as we journey through life we all have lessons to learn, some harsher than others – and the wounds of betrayal are deep and painful.

These lessons are there to challenge you, because if you haven't made a mistake and if you haven't had to overcome obstacles and difficulties in your life then you won't have learned anything. Having lived through it you now have survival skills you didn't have before, and these will enable you to protect yourself if you ever encounter betrayal again.

It's possible to have the joy and passion you deserve in your life, but first you need to have a clear view of what you want and who you are, not who you think you should be and not what you think other people expect you to be. Once you know that, you can then believe in yourself again and learn to trust. I'm not talking about trusting someone else, I'm talking about trusting yourself enough to know that you can turn the wounds into wisdom and cope with anything life throws at you. You can have the confidence and courage to overcome any obstacles in your path by having the belief that you can and will ultimately get through it.

Many people live their lives without passion, and some even substitute the things that should matter for the superficial, i.e. lots of money, up market homes, and expensive cars. They constantly seek approval and need to be liked. No amount of money or power makes the man or woman. Learning the lessons and challenging your spirit go a long way to making for a colorful life as opposed to a grey existence. So the next time you're faced with a difficulty think of it only as an opportunity and remember the old adage: "There's no gain without pain."

There are four fundamental requirements that are not negotiable when entering a relationship:

1. Respect

We all know that respect is something to be earned. To be a respectful person is to have character, integrity, principles and compassion. These are qualities you want in yourself and should demand in your mate.

2. Trust

Trust is feeling safe in the knowledge that you can share your vulnerabilities, be totally honest and know you won't be exposed or betrayed in any way.

3. Love

Love is to care for the feelings of the person we love above our own. It is to honor and hold dear, to take pleasure in and treasure. It is selfless.

4. Commitment

Commitment is a pledge, a promise and a covenant not to be broken. It requires loyalty, responsibility and strict adherence to the principles your relationship stands for.

Key points

- Don't make the fatal mistake of thinking you can change someone.
- Don't consider someone as a partner if you don't like what they show you in the beginning. It will still be there in the end.
- Make sure they have all the physical, emotional, mental, moral and spiritual dynamics you need before you enter into a relationship with someone.
- Finally, don't enter into a relationship with anyone you cannot trust or admire.

  So to end, my advice is to be the very best you can be, expect nothing but the very best in return, and you will get the best out of life in the future.

If it all goes wrong

- When people treat you badly, it's because you let them.
- Take responsibility for where you went wrong.
- Accept you've made a mistake.
- Don't carry resentment.
- Take time to heal.
- Put a high price on yourself, because if you don't you'll only get what you think you deserve, not what you are worth.
- Never say never again because true love does exist and if you close yourself off you might not recognize it when it comes.
- It's never too late to find real love: five years of real love at 70 is better than 20 years of the wrong love.

CHAPTER 16

Julia's story: Epilogue

Late one afternoon about a year before Andrew died, I was watching the end of a movie on the TV in my office; after all, even private investigators have to have some time out occasionally .The film, as I recall, was A Good Year, with Russell Crowe and Marion Cotillard, and the final scene was playing out. Right as Russell looked longingly at his true love and the music swelled as it does, Andrew walked into the office with a quizzical look on his face. "See that, Andrew?" I said, gesturing at the TV. "That's what I want." I remember he gave me a look as if to say "Dream on!"

Since our marriage had ended, I had been alone for almost ten years. For most of that time I had been content running my business and renovating my home; it seemed to be enough. But people I met seemed to be forever asking me whether I had a partner, or whether there was any love interest in my life these days. "You need to lower the bar, Julia; he won't come knocking at your door," I remember somebody saying to me. I'd always believed that one day, somehow, somewhere, I'd find true love, but I have to admit I was beginning to wonder if my faith had been misplaced.

Well, you know what? The man I was looking for actually did knock on my door one day, in the form of a television producer called Steve. Funny thing was we had met a few years before when 60 Minutes interviewed me. For some reason Steve just kept phoning me after he came to my door – the way he tells it now he decided there and then that he was going to have me no matter what. Of course it took a little longer before I clicked that there was something going on with this guy. He'd been on his own for a long time too, so both of us were very shy and unsure of what to do when someone becomes more and more important to you. Anyway, to cut a long story short, and to the relief of our friends and family, Steve and I finally became an item. Just a year later we were married.

That day, our wedding at the beautiful country home of Steve's sister was the first time I had been a bride, worn a wedding dress and had a wedding ring placed on my finger. I danced with my new father in-law and laughed with my family and friends into the night. It all felt wonderfully new and exciting, because I can honestly say it's the only time I have been married for the right reasons. I married Steve for no other reason except love, because he is the love of my life. I'm in my fifties now and I'm the happiest I've ever been in my life.

The daughter I gave birth to at 15 lives next door with her husband and two teenage sons. My daughters and I are very close. I still live in my seaside cottage, although my friends tell me it's more like a palace now. I share it with Steve and our thee dogs Soggy, Vida and Plum and I just wish my parents were here to see how happy I am and how good my life is. They've been gone a long time now, but I know they would be very proud that after all these years their daughter has learned the greatest lesson of all: when it comes to finding true love, you only need to get lucky once.

www.ingramcontent.com/pod-product-compliance
Lightning Source LLC
Chambersburg PA
CBHW070631160426
43194CB00009B/1427